U0142388

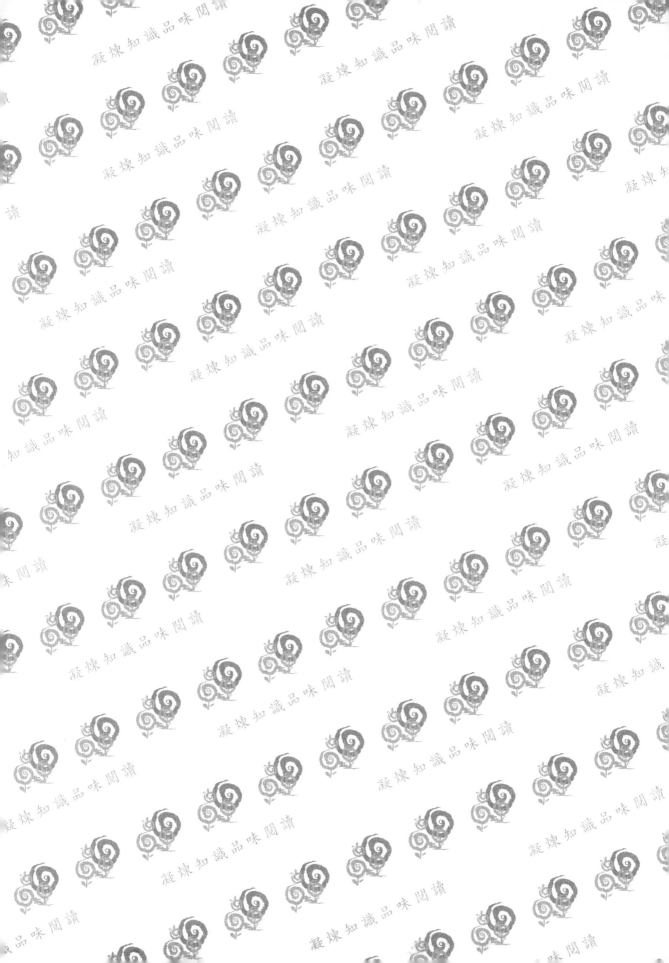

1. 圖2

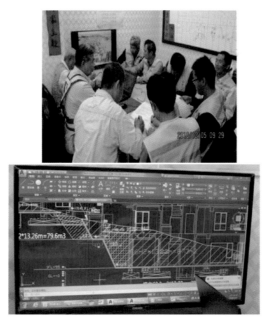

圖 2 山坡地開挖安全的風險評估討論

2. 圖3

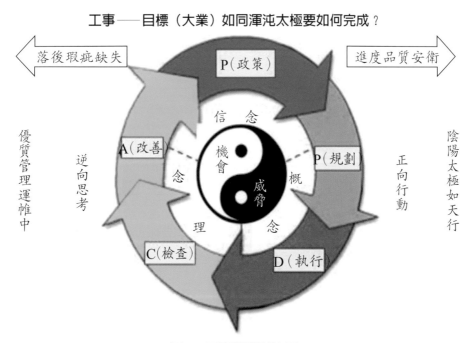

圖 3 工事管理道法圖

3. 圖4

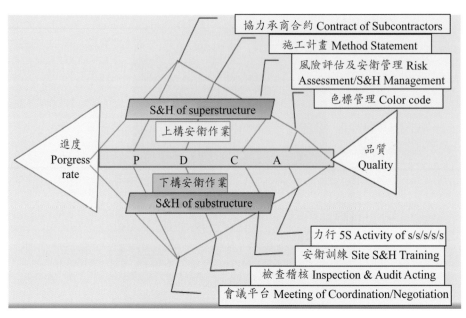

圖4　進度、安全、品質魚形圖

4. 圖5

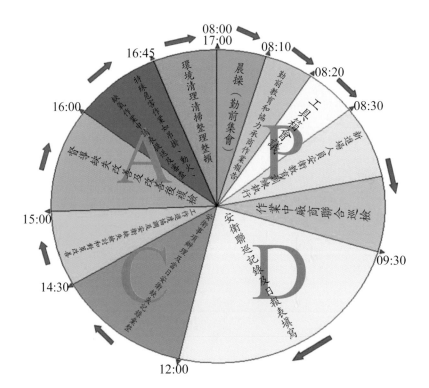

圖5　精實管理作業日晷圖

5. 圖12

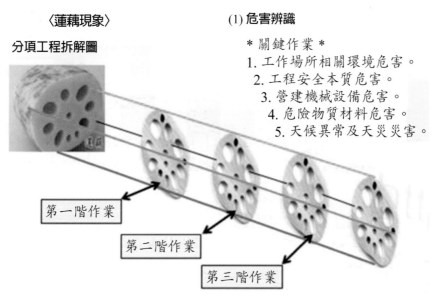

〈蓮藕現象〉

分項工程拆解圖

第一階作業

第二階作業

第三階作業

(1) **危害辨識**

＊關鍵作業＊
1. 工作場所相關環境危害。
2. 工程安全本質危害。
3. 營建機械設備危害。
4. 危險物質材料危害。
5. 天候異常及天災災害。

圖12　分項工程作業拆解階梯圖

6. 圖13

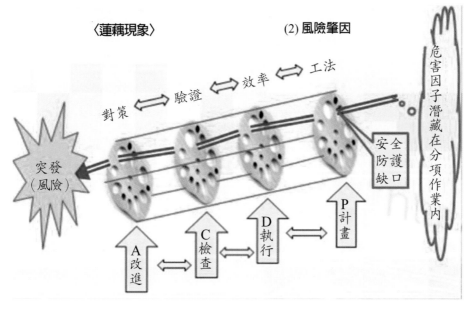

〈蓮藕現象〉

(2) **風險肇因**

危害因子潛藏在分項作業內

對策 ⇔ 驗證 ⇔ 效率 ⇔ 工法

突發
(風險)

安全
防護
缺口

A
改進　C
檢查　D
執行　P
計畫

圖13　危害與風險關係圖

7. 圖14

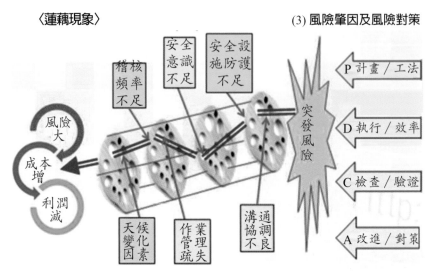

〈蓮藕現象〉　　　　　　　　　　　　　　(3) 風險肇因及風險對策

圖14　風險肇因及對策圖

8. 圖15

公司名稱	部門	評估日期	評估人員	審核者							
營造股份有限公司		108.03.01									
1.作業／流程名稱	2.危害辨識及後果（危害可能造成後果之情境描述）	3.現有防護設施	4.評估風險			5.降低風險所採取之控制措施	6.控制後預估風險		
			嚴重度	可能性	風險等級		嚴重度	可能性	風險等級
施工架工程／吊運工程／人員	人員於吊掛作業中無相關掛服被開例罰單	入場前操作手及吊掛手證書（照）資料確認	S2 (P2)	P3 (S3)		1.每日作業危害告知。2.作業時確實巡視、督導，若有違反，停止作業至違規事項消除後得復工。	S2 (P2)	P1 (S1)	

圖15　營建工程風險評量作業所使用的標準版格式

9. 圖16

風險矩陣 Risk Matrix		可能性等級 Probability			
		P4	P3	P2	P1
嚴重度 等級 Severity	S4	16	12	8	4
	S3	12	9	6	3
	S2	8	6	4	2
	S1	4	3	2	1
16—高度危急風險				立即停工改善	
12～8—危險風險				立即改善	
6～3—高度風險				改善時間一日	
2—中度風險				改善時間二日	
1—低度風險				改善時間三日	

圖16　風險矩陣分析的嚴重度等級及可能性等級包含處理對策

10. 圖22

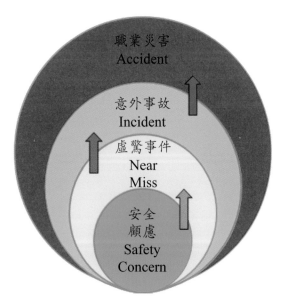

圖22　職業災害發生的進階要因圖

11. 圖23

・斷鏈對策
・每日落實 PDCA 及 5S 管理機制
・力行缺失改善
・研議有效對策

・斷鏈對策
・作業環境巡查頻率增加／回報同仁 5W／1H 採取有效防護措施

職業災害 Accident
安全顧慮 Safety concern
意外事故 Incident
虛驚事件 Near Miss

・斷鏈對策
・作業區域的人及設施需符合法規要求全方位防護

・斷鏈對策
・立即停止作業
・現場說明標準作業程序及後續觀察

圖 23　防止災害進階發生的斷鏈對策

12. 圖46

圖 46　覆工鈑上方需規劃安全通道以防止材料亂置有飛落之虞

13.圖47

圖 47　水平支撐上方需規劃設置人員安全通道及安全護欄

14.圖59

圖 59　電梯豎井需設置安全柵欄及警告標示

15.圖64

圖64　樓梯間進行泥作粉刷時，採用防墜網替代安全護欄。

16.圖67

圖67　施工架組裝完成後，與結構體的間隙為防止人員墜落，每一層施工架需張掛長條防墜網。

17.圖68

施工架延伸配件──三角架及輔助板料

圖68　施工架組裝完成後，與結構體的間隙為防止人員墜落，可跳層施作延伸平台。

18.圖72

圖72　鋼骨結構配合固定式起重機（塔吊）作業的態樣

19.圖76

圖76　鋼構作業人員使用背負式安全帶雙勾掛確保作業安全

20.圖77

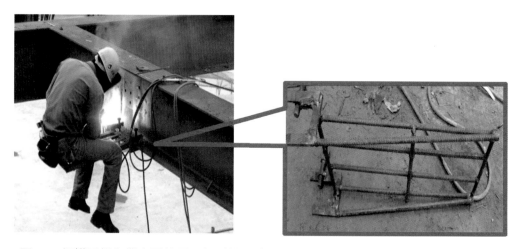

圖77　鋼構電焊作業人員使用叉架（簡易式坐板），其下方必須有安全防墜網張掛。

21.圖78

圖 78　鋼構作業人員使用安全工作架時，必須使用勾掛安全帶。

22.圖81

圖 81　鋼構作業為防止墜落事件，可於鋼結構外側加掛全幕式防墜網。

23.圖92

圖 92　工地分電箱均採上鎖管理暨箱蓋張貼維修相關人員電話及明確標示

24.圖94

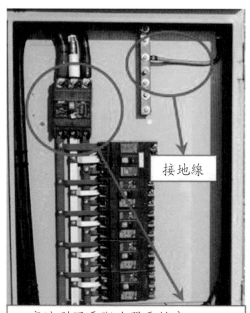

未使用 U 型或
O 型壓接端子

高速型漏電斷路器靈敏度 30mA
0.1 秒以內就能完成啟斷動作

延長線搭接時需使用 U 型或 O 型
壓接端子

圖 94　依法規規定工地臨時分電箱內總開關及分路開關的標準器具配置

25. 圖112

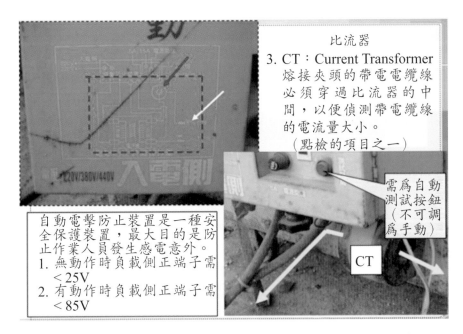

比流器
3. CT：Current Transformer
熔接夾頭的帶電電纜線
必須穿過比流器的中
間，以便偵測帶電纜線
的電流量大小。
（點檢的項目之一）

需為自動
測試按鈕
（不可調
為手動）

CT

自動電擊防止裝置是一種安
全保護裝置，最大目的是防
止作業人員發生感電意外。
1. 無動作時負載側正端子需
   ＜25V
2. 有動作時負載側正端子需
   ＜85V

圖112　交流電焊機作業前的點檢，是要確認自動電擊防止裝置作動必須正常及電力線必須
　　　　穿過比流器。

26. 圖113

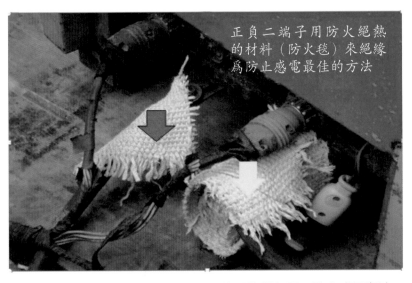

正負二端子用防火絕熱
的材料（防火毯）來絕緣
為防止感電最佳的方法

圖113　交流電焊機負載側的正負端子均需絕緣包覆，防止感電意外。

27.圖126

圖 126　地下室地樑鋼筋紮結作業時突然倒塌造成職災死亡事故

28.圖139

圖 139　施工架壁連座的間距垂直線在 9M 以內及水平線在 8M 以內。

29. 圖140

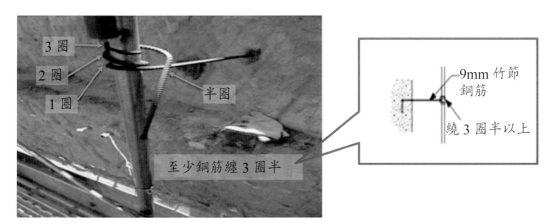

3圈

2圈

1圈

半圈

至少鋼筋纏3圈半

9mm 竹節鋼筋

繞3圈半以上

圖140　施工架與結構體繫牆桿可採用 #3 鋼筋纏繞 3 圈半後，下摺固定。

30. 圖142

圖142　防止施工架倒塌與鋼骨結構下翼鈑繫牆桿安全的作法

31.圖146

圖 146　遵照環保法令第 11 條工地抑制粉塵，施工架必須張掛防塵網。

32.圖165

圖 165　樓板高度超過 3.5M 時，鋼管支撐需設置縱向及橫向的水平繫條。

33.圖171

圖 171　結構柱牆及樑採鋁製系統模板組立完成並採斜撐的態樣

34.圖217

圖 217　現場使用軌道式電動整平機進行混凝土平整作業

35. 圖238

圖238　電焊火花碰到達到飽和揮發性溶劑的泥土瞬間起火

36. 圖251

圖251　作業前檢點相關設施（如三腳架配捲揚防墜器、通風換氣設施、個人防護具、送電開關含漏電斷路器、長鋁梯）及其他等

37.圖258

圖 258　入坑人員經由吊升三腳架緩緩入坑作業

38.圖293

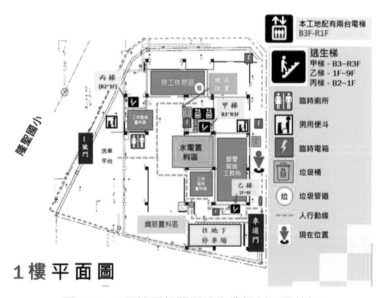

圖 293　工區範圍相關假設作業規劃配置執行

39.圖329

圖 329　每月定期檢查現場的鋼索，如符合安全規定，則依每月色標噴漆識別。

40.圖330

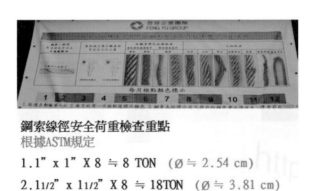

鋼索線徑安全荷重檢查重點
根據ASTM規定

1.1" x 1" X 8 ≒ 8 TON　(∅ ≒ 2.54 cm)

2.1₁/₂" x 1₁/₂" X 8 ≒ 18TON　(∅ ≒ 3.81 cm)

3.16/8" x 16/8" X 8 ≒ 24 TON　(∅ ≒ 4.4 cm)

圖 330　色標管理：鋼索經檢查合格後，依當月顏色噴漆作為安全辨識。

41.圖386

圖386　現場振動液壓打樁機繼續施打中間柱的態樣

42.圖391

圖391　圍令與 H 型鋼樁之間的空隙需用混凝土填滿

43.圖410

圖410　擋土排樁與第一層水平支撐接合的態樣

44.圖414

圖414　基於安全考量，擋土排樁外側的側壓力逐圍令增加一層加勁的態樣。

45.圖416

圖416　擋土排樁與四種不同高程的水平支撐接合之態樣

46.圖444

圖444　水平支撐材料進場需採兩點吊掛作業

47.圖460

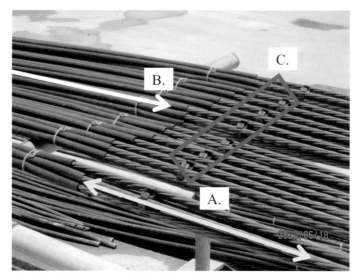

圖460　鋼鍵長度可分前段叫錨碇段（A.），後段叫自由段（B.）及鋼鍵環型夾片（C.）

48.圖461

圖461　鑽堡機依照設計孔徑、深度、角度進行旋轉及衝擊完成引孔的態樣

49.圖472

圖 472　擋土壁之開挖面進行安裝第一段橫擋的態樣

50.圖477

圖 477　施加預力構件說明：1. 台座；2. 承壓鈑；3. 千斤頂；4. 握線夾頭；5. 楔子夾片；6. 鋼鍵

51.圖479

圖 479　擋土壁完成第二段橫擋的作業及部分錨頭完成預力施作的態樣

52.圖488

圖 488　建築資訊模型是當今可視性影像達成溝通的最佳工具

53.圖532

圖532　工地設置人臉辨識器，落實進場人員管制作業的態樣。

54.圖537

圖537　察覺工地發生嚴重缺失時，除立即停工外，並現場解說要求立即將缺失改善的態樣。

55.圖554

圖 554 電梯井的防墜柵欄及背負式安全帶勾掛使用鋼索的態樣

56.圖567

圖 567 施工架的上下設備，其防塵網採用不同顏色以示區別的態樣。

57.圖577

圖 577 施工期間防止室外雨水由樓梯間進入室內，其對策之二是室內樓梯旁跳層設置導水槽。

58.圖598

圖 598 現場上構鋼柱與逆打鋼柱採用鋼構連結調整器接合固定

59. 圖707

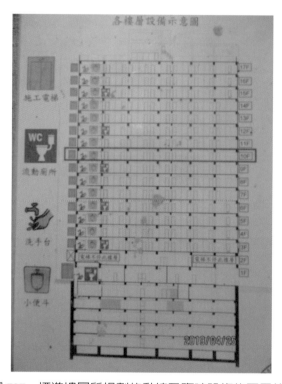

圖 707　標準樓層所規劃的動線及臨時設施的圖示位置圖

60. 圖709

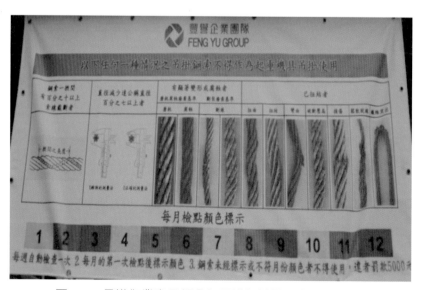

圖 709　吊掛作業索具部分每月進行檢點及色標管理的態樣

61.圖728

圖 728　鋼柱的底鈑及預埋螺栓固定於角鋼支撐架上端的態樣

62.圖754

圖 754　現場彩鋼鈑安裝人員均穿戴及勾掛背負式安全帶作業的態樣

63.圖785

圖 785　結構鋼網系統模板拆模後，牆面呈現平滑的態樣。

64.圖793

圖 793　現場牆壁面板依照規範裝置鋼管斜撐，防止倒塌意外發生的態樣。

工事安全衛生精實管理

彭元傑 ———— 著

五南圖書出版公司 印行

The Skilled Lean Management of Safety & Health for Construction

推薦序

在豐譽企業團隊的同仁都暱稱元傑君為「彭哥」。

豐譽聯合前身為「德寶」，重整期間，調整體質並重建公司文化，回歸創業時「以人為本」之中心思想。為整頓公司工地安全衛生管理系統、安衛意識及工作習慣，特聘請彭兄前來襄助。元傑參與多項國家重大建設，與國際知名營建公司合作的經驗尤其可貴。

彭哥與公司核心幹部協同重建營造施工的工作習慣、建立標準作業流程及工地安全衛生管理準則。

豐譽（德寶）團隊勵精圖治、去蕪存菁，一步一腳印的經營，歷經十年而浴火重生、脫胎換骨。成為一家負責、熱情、有創意的專業服務團隊。

安全衛生管理也獲得許多獎項：

2020　第十四屆勞動部優良工程金安獎佳作——台糖沙崙住宅園區

2020　臺南市空氣品質維護暨低碳節能績優單位——台糖沙崙住宅園區

2020　新竹市政府營造工程道路洗掃認養——工研院光復院區研發大樓（二期）

2019　臺南市建築工程圍籬綠美化競賽特優——台糖沙崙住宅園區

2018　新竹市優良環保工程——工研院光復院區研發大樓（二期）

2016　新北市建築工程圍籬綠美化佳作——新光人壽新板傑仕堡 A 基地

2015　嘉義市「年度優良工地楷模」積分第一名——新光人壽嘉義中興大樓

2014　交通部全國交通工程環境影響評估追蹤考核協助業主取得第二名——高鐵苗栗站興建工程台灣高鐵「2014 年度職業安全衛生管理績效優異廠商」

2011　職業安全衛生管理績效優異廠商——台灣高鐵核心系統變電站

彭哥以畢生經驗及豐富學理基礎，將建築營建工程安全衛生管理做有系統的分析及實務管理要項，並以各種圖表及現場照片提示，供讀者參考，以提攜後進，提升整體營建工程安衛水準，值得讚佩！

　　彭哥囑我作序，樂於接受，期待工程從業人員廣為流傳，詳以閱讀，提升工地安全意識，達到「進度起領、安全優先、品質極致」的目標。

國策顧問／豐譽企業團隊榮譽董事長

賴悅顏 手書

推薦序

　　元傑投入營造產業已有 38 年資歷，經歷台北捷運、101 大樓、台灣高鐵等重大建設，任職期間在數個國際知名營造外商擔任職業安全衛生主管，於 2010 年來到豐譽企業團隊，元傑對於安全工作的熱情及誠懇堅定的態度，深獲工地現場施工人員的認同，也感染公司同事，建立公司全員重視安全的共識及職業安全管理制度，元傑打下的職安基礎，讓公司營業規模得以穩健的快速成長。元傑在公司年紀較長，同事習慣稱呼「彭哥」，「彭哥」在豐譽已是「安全規章」的代名詞。

　　元傑在公司服務期間已出版 85 期的豐譽安保快訊，把新聞中的工安意外事件、氣候變化的因應、職安標準作法及公司政策透過快訊即時傳達給同事，職安工作之外，能把畢生經驗傳承給產業界更多的工程後輩們，是他內心的志業，《工事安全衛生精實管理》一書，裡面有精闢的管理心法，清晰的職安工作架構及管理系統，透過實務相片呈現，讓讀者容易掌握傳達的實質內容，有助於營造工程從業者快速建立職業安全的管理思維及知識。

　　從事營造行業我們先自許有能力維護大家的安全，這是和元傑一起共事的心得，過程雖然辛苦，但「照顧大家的安全」是一份很有意義、有福報的好工作，而這本書適合職安有心人珍藏，隨時翻閱參考。

豐譽企業團隊董事長

謝信燁

序言

　　我爲什麽要寫這本書？淺顯的說，作者多年來謹記國策顧問暨榮譽董事長賴悅顏先生的一句話「以人爲本、關懷生命」，基於此堅定不移的信念及能力所及的前提下開始伏案運筆，寫出職人的安全衛生實務管理心得。

　　作者38年間投入營建業領域，此期間參與多項國家重大建設，如臺北捷運木柵線、文湖線初期土木工程及後期機電系統工程，以及臺北101金融大樓地下結構工程興建。作者於2000年1月加入承建台灣高鐵第一標C280標（嘉義水上至臺南官田）韓國三星營建團隊安全衛生管理成員。外商服務期間前後共計9年，如日商大豐／日商奧村組／加拿大商龐巴迪等公司。

　　有鑑於日商及加商的安全衛生管理機制各有其優點，作者遂擇取雙方上乘優質的管理機制，並融合多年來工地實務經驗所頓悟的心法。在職業安全衛生法令的範疇下，開始寫出如何提升工程界安衛管理達到零職災的目標做努力。

　　二年來利用工作餘暇之時，進行整理、伏案潤筆及檢校修正，以達到新書內容言簡意賅及圖示說明簡潔明瞭，使讀者能在有效閱讀及理解通達的氛圍下，吸取本書各章節的管理精華內容。尤其工程的「施工風險評估」，是工程安全衛生管理的重要課題。執行上必須落實每日安衛管理機制的任何作業，譬如預知作業前危害因子的存在，經過分析及評量後研議出對策，採用正確有效的工法，把高風險降成低風險的安全作業環境，達到可以管控的殘餘風險及零風險，才能達標工地零職災的安衛政策。

　　本書的關鍵實務安衛管理做法、插圖的中英文解說和安全自主管理的執行做法等，可謂本書的亮點所在，在此分享給已從事工程安全衛生管理的執行者及有興趣的參與者，均可以把本書作爲工具書參考。

　　本書特點如下：

1. 補強工地安全衛生管理者的執行做法及高效率的展現，和緊急意外事故發生時，災害問題因果的判斷、救災處理及解決的關鍵性做法。

2. 本書所蒐集的實務照片及中英解說，可以使讀者非常容易通達了解及運用。

3. 工程施工風險評估的四步驟，其章節均有詳細篇幅說明，祈望讀者們閱讀了解後，在作業上能達到事半功倍的效果。

　　編著期間謝謝家人的支持，也由衷感謝榮譽董事長賴悅顏先生對本著作相關內容的指導建議，使內容更加精實。感謝董事長兼總經理謝佶燁先生、董事邱建揚先生、葉技師奕昌先生等長官，平日給作者就安衛執行層面的大力支持，讓作者毫無懸念和其他同仁們全力以赴，終於奪得勞動部109年全國優良工程金安獎的殊榮。另外在安全衛生管理的生涯中，也感謝摯友黃董事長熾勳先生、日本好友菅原修及田中啟一的建言支持，及林馥嫻和應政華同仁的協助，才得以完成本著作。特此謹致由衷之謝忱。

＊太極意象論風險管理

　　易經素來是作為窮盡天地奧祕的哲理書，對成卦過程的分析，根本說來，也是對天地開闢的概述。

　　易經中的「太極」與「道」字相通，正因萬物由「道」所生，因此萬物變化均由太極化成兩儀、四象、八卦。

人法地，地法天，
天法道，道法自然。

無極生太極，
太極生兩儀，
兩儀生四象，
四象生八卦，
八卦生六十四卦，
六十四卦生宇宙萬象。

　　結論是：太極＝陰＋陽＝道。

　　道，即宇宙運行，日月氣候自然變化的法則。

＊安全衛生管理道法意涵

安全衛生管理機制（安全衛生管理道法）：意謂工程安衛管理要先根據道（亦執行機制如 P.D.C.A。PLAN：規劃／DO：執行／CHECK：檢查／ACTION：改善）。在機制運用的**法**（準則如 POLICY：政策／ACT：法令）的確立，猶如天體運行似太極陰陽有日夜之分，既成規律，日復一日據於落實。工程師們才能了解感受此優質安衛管理機制的核心價值。

營建工程於施工期間，包含許多的不同工程分項作業，如何把眾多分流工項經由優質管理機制匯集成主流，減少管理作業的障礙，執行過程中明確的管理目標（年度零職災）是非常重要的。每日 **P＞D＞C＞A** 機制循環落實是必要的作法。簡言之，任何分項作業均需採用源流管理及使用 **P.D.C.A** 有效能的管理機制，因為它是達標「工程零職災」的重要起手式。

施工風險評估的重要，亦即任何營建工程在建造期程，基於有限的時間、組織人力、材料成本等考量，為達到進度如期、安全無虞、品質如式的目標。就工程管理而言，必須採用高效率且零職災的優質安衛管理機制，才可以達到如期完工的目標。

＊施工風險評估的重要

各類型工程不論是地上的超高摩天大樓，或地下結構工程及隧道潛盾工程於施工中，均有潛存的風險，風險的管控得當，對承攬商可謂是**機會**，相對的，管控失當就是威脅。

常言道：日暈三更雨，月暈午時風，表示宇宙自然的陰陽變化，引用到工程管理層面做比較，專案工程就是一個大業，如「**進度如期**」、「**品質如式**」、「**造價如度**」、「**安全無虞**」及「**符合環保**」這五個必要條件，在施工期間均需同時達成，這有賴於工程優質管理機制的落實。落實完全的結果就是創造利潤，可譬白日光明

所謂是「機會」。相反地管理未落實完全，施工期間屢生意外事故的結果就造成成本的增加，此情況可譬闇黑就是「威脅」。

　　風險如太極，必需用科學而有系統的方法，即業主、設計單位及營建承攬商在規劃各分項作業時，必需納入施工風險評估的概念和 **5W/1H** 及天候的關鍵因素，研討出各類工項潛在危害因子必需排除的有效對策。如無法預期突發性的施工意外事故發生，也要研擬一套有效的應變機制，給予遵行辦理以降低風險的負面衝擊。然而風險評估作業是風險管控中最容易達成管控的目的。

　　遂工程風險管理者必需在事前進行辨識、事中進行分析和評量、釐訂改善對策採取各種有效措施和方法，消除或減少風險事件發生的各種可能性及嚴重度，防制職災事故的發生。

＊「進度起領、安全優先、品質極致」

　　此口訣心法著重於實務性工程安全衛生優質管理信念的深耕。此機制運用在不同的排程階段，即使分項工程作業性質不同，但熟稔運用此管理機制，執行的成果是可預期的，亦即達成零職災的終極目標。

　　任何工程都有風險，開工後，最重要的是把主要工程分項作業的程序，拆解（所謂三階層）至最低階層的作業，進行危害辨識及風險分析，並研討現有的防護設施是否足以防制，更進一步則採取風險評量，研擬出對策予以排除，因此作業前落實完整的分析，找出潛在危害因子。再採用優質安衛管理作業機制，將此隱患降低或消弭，針對營建工程而言，作業環境及設施達到安全衛生的作法，均有利於進度及品質的達成。目前少許業界在承造工程作業中，針對施工風險評估作業，均採用建築資訊模型，簡稱 BIM（Building Information Modeling）的作業方式，來確認暨執行最安全的工法。

＊「達標零職災」

　　營建工程施作期間採用優質管理機制的效能，廣義的說，可用立竿見影來比喻。本書內容屬營建工程實務性安衛管理工具書，圖片部分並採用中英文版方式說明，其主要目的是讓有心從事職安衛管理的後學者及有志進入外商服務的後進者一個導引及參考。書中中英文內容部分因準備倉促，如有疏漏不足之處，尚祈各位長官、同業先進指導及不吝賜教，後學將虛心潛學改正，並對各位大德善舉感德為禱。

作者介紹

彭元傑

服務單位：豐譽企業團隊（豐譽營造股份有限公司／豐譽聯合工程股份有限公司／上裕開發股份有限公司）

職　　稱：安保中心副理（民國99年9月～迄今）

1. 學歷：國立台北工專（改制國立台北科技大學）畢業

2. 著作：營建安全衛生與實務管理（1993台北國際商學出版）

3. 語言：英文聽、說、寫、流利。日語聽、說、寫可及閩客語。

4. 經歷：

(1) 日勝生集團新店美和市住宅專案工程安衛主任
（1年8個月／98.1～99.8年）

(2) 加拿大龐巴迪公司文湖線捷運核心機電系統工程
安衛經理（2年6個月／95.6～97.12年）

(3) 日商奧村組營造公司台北市捷運新蘆線地下段潛盾工程
安衛經理（1年4個月／94.1～95.5年）

(4)日商大豐營造公司高鐵S220標新竹六家車站工程

安衛經理（2年4個月／91.8～93.12年）

(5)韓國三星營造（股）公司台灣高速鐵路C280標工程

安衛經理（2年7個月／89.1～91.7年）

(6)達欣工程股份有限公司承建台北國際金融101大樓

地下結構工程安衛主任.（5年／84.1～88.12年）

(7)省營唐榮鐵工廠營建部幫工程司兼勞工安全暨品質管制

中心主任（13年6個月／70.7～83.12年）

5. 授業學校：

(1)臺北市職業安全衛生學院講師

(2)文化大學進修推廣部講師

6. 國外學術研討專題演講：

香港職業安全衛生協會發函邀請彭員於海峽兩岸及香港、澳門地區職業安全健康學術研討會專題論文報告。

共計（第19屆2011.11.&第26屆2018.09.）計二次

A.2011年受邀赴香港專題報告（建造業安全如何達成）

B.2018年受邀赴香港專題報告（建造業安全優質管理新趨勢）

7. 歷年來獲得的獎項

2020　　第十四屆勞動部優良工程金安獎佳作：
　　　　台糖沙崙住宅園區工程

2020　　臺南市空氣品質維護暨低碳節能績優單位：
　　　　台糖沙崙住宅園區工程

2020　　新竹市政府營造工程道路洗掃認養：
　　　　工研院光復院區研發大樓（二期）工程

2019　　臺南市建築工程圍籬綠美化競賽特優：
　　　　台糖沙崙住宅園區工程

2018　　新竹市優良環保工程：
　　　　工研院光復院區研發大樓（二期）工程

2016　　新北市建築工程圍籬綠美化佳作：
　　　　新光人壽新板傑仕堡A基地工程

2015　　嘉義市「年度優良工地楷模」積分第一名：
　　　　新光人壽嘉義中興大樓工程

2014　　交通部全國交通工程環境影響評估追蹤考
　　　　核協助業主高鐵公司取得第二名
　　　　台灣高鐵苗栗站興建工程
　　　　「2014年度職業安全衛生管理績效優異廠商」

2011　　職業安全衛生管理績效優異廠商：
　　　　台灣高鐵核心系統變電站工程

目錄

第一章 ｜ 工事風險 **Risk of Construction** ·················· *1*

　　1-1　風險的肇因 Cause of risk.　　　　　　　　2

　　1-2　風險評估的重要性 What important of risk assessment.　3

第二章 ｜ 精實管理 **Lean Management** ···················· *5*

　　2-1　精實管理的三原則 Guidelines of lean management.　6

　　2-2　工事管理的道法 Essential the way of construction

　　　　 management.　　　　　　　　　　　　　6

第三章 ｜ 全員安衛的意義 **Meaning of Engineers in Total**

Safety & Health ··············· *13*

　　3-1　安全的重要 What safety is important！　　　14

第四章 ｜ 工程風險管理 **Risk Management of Construction** ······ *17*

　　4-1　安全與危險的區別 Distinction between safety & danger.

　　　　　　　　　　　　　　　　　　　　　18

　　4-2　本質安全的重要性 Importance of intrinsic safety.　18

　　4-3　解析施工風險評估作業（蓮藕現象）Analyzing

　　　　 operation of risk assessment of construction

　　　　 (Phenomenon of Lotus Root).　　　　　21

　　4-4　意外災害暨緊急應變 Disaster occurred with emergency

　　　　 response.　　　　　　　　　　　　　25

4-5　工地全方位緊急救援演練 Drill of emergency rescue in comprehensive at site.　32

第五章 ｜ 工地高風險作業的管理防制及對策 **Crucial Controlling & Strategy Were to The High Risk Operation at Work Site** ················· *37*

5-1　何謂職業災害 What occupational disaster is?　38

5-2　墜落防止 Fall prevention.　40

5-3　感電災害防制 Accident of electric shock prevention.　65

5-4　倒塌崩塌防制的關鍵要領 Crucial skill of prevention for collapse & tumble down.　81

5-5　火災防制的關鍵要領 Crucial skill of prevention for fire accident.　139

5-6　缺氧作業的關鍵要領 Crucial skill of work for hyposia operation.　152

5-7　營建工地熱危害的預防與對策 Precaution & strategy of heat illness at construction site.　161

第六章 ｜ 新建工程安全衛生實務管理精要作業 **Crucial Operation of Safety & Health Management to New Construction Project** ················· *177*

6-1　動土前作業要點 Essential work operation before the ceremony of ground breaking.　178

6-2　開工動土後工區規劃作業要點 Essential work planning & operation after ceremony of ground breaking & commence.　179

6-3　地下結構分項工程安全衛生規劃暨執行要點 Essential

work planning & executed of safety & health for the sectoral work of substructures. 196

6-4　地上結構分項工程安全衛生規劃暨執行要點 Essential work planning & executed of safety & health for the sectoral work of superstructures. 277

6-5　建築鋼筋混凝土結構工程 Structure construction of architecture was reinforced concrete. 282

6-6　鋼骨鋼筋混凝土結構工程 Structure construction was steel reinforced concrete. 327

6-7　鋼骨結構工程 Steel structure construction. 396

6-8　創改型系統模板工程 Creation & improvement type of formwork system construction. 432

第一章　工事風險 Risk of Construction

1-1　風險的肇因 Cause of risk.

1-2　風險評估的重要性 What important of risk assessment.

1-1 風險的肇因 Cause of risk

風險一詞具有許多不同的含義，就營建工程而言，在一個特定的區域環境及有限的工期內，由於人員、機械及材料等管理疏失，而造成人員意外事故、工程停工及成本損失的可能性，均可謂之風險。

圖 1 各類型態的風險均潛存於工程作業中

Figure 1. Many different potential risks were hidden in the construction operation.

風險管理是一個主動的管理過程，進行各類分項作業，系統化的階層分析，並涵蓋所有可預見的危害辨識和相關風險的分析及評量，落實可行的對策及持續改善的機制。在風險評估過程的每個步驟中，都需要與業主代表、設計單位及相關承包商進行協商。通過專業人員的經驗、知識和想法，共同識別所有危害，並選擇有效的控制措施，達成零職災的目標。

1-2 風險評估的重要性 What important of risk assessment

圖 2 山坡地開挖安全的風險評估討論

Figure 2. Risk assessment was hold to discuss the safety of hilly land operation.

　　一個安全衛生的工作場所，必須是施工團隊全員用心及所謂的精實管理機制所經營出來的。好的營建安全工地絕不是偶然的。工事進行中的**作業前**，工程管理者必須考慮在工作場所範圍可能會發生什麼問題以及可能產生的後果。**作業中**利用優質的自主管理機制來了解作業現場危害因子發生的前因後果，**作業後**彙集全部缺失研討出可行改善對策，必須盡一切可能來消除或最小化所謂風險的發生。風險評估作業中的風險矩陣內包含**嚴重度**及**可能性**，可以幫助設計團隊及施工承商確定：

- 風險有多嚴重是否超出預期？
- 現有的控制措施是否有效防制？
- 應採取什麼對策或措施來控制風險？
- 需要採取多緊急的措施降低風險？
- 殘餘風險要如何因應或消除？

第二章　精實管理 Lean Management

2-1　精實管理的三原則 Guidelines of lean management.

2-2　工事管理的道法 Essential the way of construction management.

2-1 精實管理的三原則 Guidelines of Lean Management

一、進度起領 Lead of progress rate

　　營建工程現今趨勢已翻轉成高風險且非常嚴峻的作業場所，工程從業人員都了解本質安全的重要，實務執行上必須依據作業排程的項目為標準，所謂事前採用正確工法的對策，才能規劃現場作業的安全措施符合法令規範要求，來達到事半功倍的效果。

二、安全優先 Priority of safety

　　常人說生命無價。工地現場的安全設施作業，是根據排程的項目來進行作業，意即作業項目明確，導引現場安衛設施的施作，提供安全的作業環境。所以從事工程的任何成員如果能善用且落實此管理機制，作業前有效的做好施工中任何階段的安全措施及設施，直到工程完成驗收交給業主，可謂功德圓滿為眾人積善造福。

三、品質極致 Superexcellence of quality

　　作業現場僱主依法提供安全的作業環境，讓所有進場作業人員，在作業中心無旁鶩，施工品質不僅符合業主合約的要求，甚至超越標準甚多，是工程管理人員所期望的成果。

2-2 工事管理的道法 Essential the Way of Construction Management

　　任何（工事／專案工程）從承攬商的立場而言，從進行專業施工項目的發包開始，所有的後續作業均可採用下述管理方式，如：進度管理／成本管理／數量管理／技術管理／品質管理／效率管理／安全管理／走動管理／色標管理／災害管理／衝突管理／設備管理／維修保養管理／色標管理／5S 管理等方式，來達成業主對本工程如期、品質如質、安全無虞的要求及目標。然工事大業如同太極，如下圖所示：

工事──目標（大業）如同渾沌太極要如何完成？

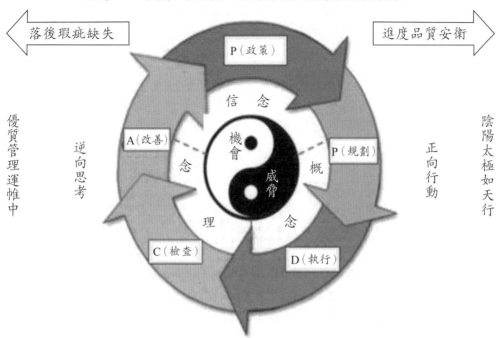

圖3　工事管理道法圖

Figure 3. Symbol was of construction management mechanism

一、進度起領的涵義 Implication of lead of progress rate

(一) 工程進度表有許多方式表達，在此我們引用一種易懂且在**項目管理**中常用到的技術就是**甘特圖**，使用甘特圖其實是一個施工項目追蹤管理的方法，通過圖形化的方式展示，顯現作業項目進度的方法。一些作業項目依賴於另一個作業的啟動，也就是說，營建各作業項目都有相互連結的關係。不論作業項目大小及數量多少，均需落實執行下面魚骨圖內所示的關鍵作業。

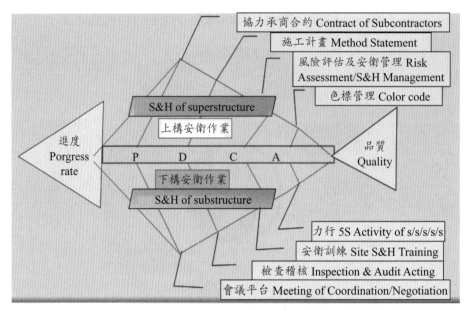

圖 4　進度、安全、品質魚形圖

Figure 4. Diagram of fish shape was to progress rate, safety & quality

（二）甘特圖中任何作業項目即是**安衛管理作業的標的**，依照該標的的特性，於作業前經由施工風險評估作業的研議來完成最適當的工法及安全防護設施。作業執行中運用 P、D、C、A 的有效管理機制來達成零職災的目標。

表 1　工程施工進度排程表

Chart1. Major scheduled of construction project

「活動中心新建工程」預定進度表

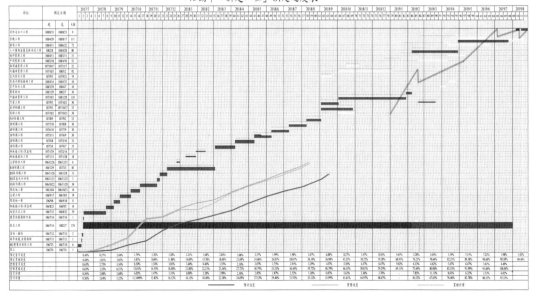

表 2　年度分項作業進度暨安全作業要點管制表

Chart2. Diagram of sector work was operated with safety management of annual schedule

全國工地夫動管理分項作業進度要點管控表

工程處工地別	狀態	工程概況基本資料	現場安全注意事項	警戒時相號誌 ○○○	105年度 1月～12月	106/107/108年度（1月～12月）	備註（潛患要點）
			作業階段要點查表		需風險注意事項		①墜落危害因子/災害 ②感電危害因子/災害 ③倒塌危害因子/災害 ④感害潛危害因子/災害 ⑤缺氧危害因子/災害 ⑥火災危害因子/災害 ⑦其他危害因子/災害
宜大工地 ok	進行中	RC　工地	①②③⑤	○	SRC(RC-B1F～5F)	A.假設及擋土支撐作業　C.1樓至結構體屋頂工程　D.裝修階段工程　B.FS～BS～鋼板臨拆除及地下室作業	
莉美興工地 ok	進行中	RC　工地	①②③④⑤	○	地下室混凝土作業	A.假設B.基礎/開挖　E.室內泥作F.水電其他　C.結構工程	
傑士堡工地 ok（工程處）	進行中	大工地	①②③④⑤	○	樓板高度約540cm	A.基礎/開挖　C.室內泥作　B.基礎/開挖　D.室內泥作　B.結構　C.結構	
士林商旅工地 ok	進行中	SRC	①②③④⑤	○	樓板高度約540cm	A.假設　E.室內泥作　D/E.室內泥作　G.完景作業	
張公館工地 ok（建景工程處）	進行中	RC　中工地	①②	○	地下室混凝土作業	B.B1樓至結構體屋頂工程　C.室內外泥作　A.地下室工程　D.清領後照作業	
名樓工地	進行中	RC　工地	①②③④⑤	○	樓板高度約700cm	A.假設B.外牆泥作　C.室內泥作　A.臨時假設開挖作業	
凱樓工地	進行中	RC　工地	①②③④⑤	○		B.基礎/開挖　E.室內泥作　C.結構	
安樂工地	進行中	RC　中工地	①②③④⑤	○	地下室混凝土作業	D/E.室內外泥作　F.水電其他　B.工地未保作業進行　C.水事主體作業	

二、安全優先的管理作法 Management method of safety priority

把工程的主要組合，如人、事、物的優勢發揮極大化，所謂流程化的管理、模組化的作業，將任何高風險的作業，首要確定施作工法或其他有效方式等。將作業環境除去不安全狀態及改正現場作業人員不安全的行為使意外風險降低，以達到零職災的目標

(一) 強化優質安全衛生管理 Enforced the priority safety & health management

1. 提升安全意識。
2. 達標安全衛生政策。
3. 訂定安全作業標準。

(二) 排除不安全作業環境 Eliminated the unsafe work condition

1. 設備安全化。
2. 作業前檢點。
3. 持續落實改善。

(三) 消除勞工不安全行為 Dispelled the unsafe behavior of workers

1.作業主管監督；2. 適當人員定位；3. 遵守作業規定。

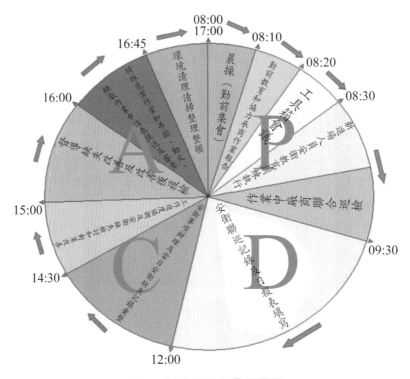

圖 5　精實管理作業日晷圖

Figure 5. Diagram of daily was operation for lean management

三、品質極致的管理作法 Management method for superexcellence quality

　　品質極致的意義是「施工品質超越它的本身價值」，如工程進度如期完工，配合施工期間零職災達標。兩個管理要項均符合合約要求的前提下，亦達成業主暨客戶最高標準的要求，完工品質是可以讓大家安心。

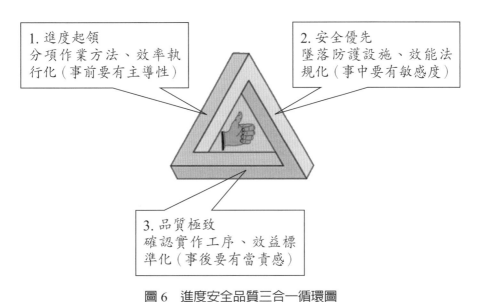

1. 進度起領
分項作業方法、效率執行化（事前要有主導性）

2. 安全優先
墜落防護設施、效能法規化（事中要有敏感度）

3. 品質極致
確認實作工序、效益標準化（事後要有當責感）

圖6　進度安全品質三合一循環圖

Figure 6. Diagram of three in one was for progress rate, safety & superexcellence quality

第三章　全員安衛的意義 Meaning of Engineers in Total Safety & Health

3-1　安全的重要 What safety is important！

3-1 安全的重要 What safety is important！

我們相信，工地是人與機械展現動能的地方，動作產生能，能可以產生建設，也可以造成意外事故，遂工程中沒有任何一件事會比安全更重要，尤其是營建業。全員全方位的參與、投入、加入安全衛生活動是非常重要的，這不僅是爲了遵守職安法的規定，除了參與和了解法規的要求，同時也是爲了能有效管控各分項作業的風險。工程師的專業知識與實務經驗是風險控制的成敗關鍵。

對風險管控作業而言，全員的參與不僅讓員工對安全衛生政策有認同感，也建立了一種相互合作的共識與默契，安全衛生的政策達標及優良績效成果，也會提升工程師對安全衛生的執行信心，並且深切體認到做好、做全是每一位工程師應有的責任。

圖 7　全員安衛管理重點示意圖

Figure 7. Images of crucial management of total safety and health

一、安全衛生政策宣言 Declaration of the policy of safety & health management

政策宣言須由公司主事者或工地主管親筆簽署並註明日期，透過宣言說明決策管理階層對安全衛生的信念與決心，來揭示事業單位的方向；追求安全衛生**年度零職災的目標**及**缺失持續改善**的決心，以符合法規的要求。

二、自動檢查表單與警告標語的使用 Using of self-checking list & warning notice

　　年度零職災的政策宣言，必須依賴系統性自動檢查表單的落實執行，其缺失數據的呈現，作為作業風險評估的依據。因此檢查表單須依照個別事業單位的需求編製。大致上，細膩度必須和作業的複雜度與風險的等級一致：尤其是風險的等級越高，作業指示就要越明確，除了系統性的文件外，事業單位還可以利用通報、海報、傳單與安全衛生刊物，通知員工特殊事件或工作進度，例如巡查的結果是否符合職安法的標準、以及職災發生後調查的結果報告等，要比一般的標語來得有效。

三、安全衛生走動管理與缺失檢討改進會議 Meeting of walking around management for safety & health with deficiencies inspected

　　工地安全衛生作業巡察與現場缺失檢討改進會議是全員安衛落實 P＞D＞C＞A 優質管理機制中非常重要的溝通平台，在會議中當責工程師及不同工項的作業主管可以與相關組員一起討論安全衛生議題，提醒他們如何面對高風險的作業與作業前、中、後各階段重要的預防作業，此舉用以補充安衛訓練作業的不足，會議的召開也可以讓所有工程師可以對安全作業的改善，提出自己的看法，經過所有參與者相互研討達成共識，防止職災的發生。

　　但是還有其他方式可以用來確保良好的溝通及參與作業，包括：定期每月安全衛生協議組織會議，在會議中可以向下傳遞工地安衛管理執行績效數據，作為工地改善安衛缺失及提升品質卓越的基準。每日的工具箱交談（Tool Box Talk）或非正式會議，在溝通中作業主管可以與作業人員一起討論安全衛生議題，提醒他們作業中風險的防制作業。

四、優質團隊應具備的正念 Excellence quality team should have correct mindfulness

　　工地主管鼓勵所有員工共同努力追求全體安全衛生目標的團隊，主管的責任包括召集團隊活動，如工具箱交談、風險評估、緊急救援演練等。它還涵蓋教導與諮詢的工作，鼓勵並支援全員參與，其中一項最重要的目的就是確保員工對分項作業前的危害辨識，以及風險的分析及評量或對策等的認知。

　　我們相信沒有任何一件事會比安全更重要，事前的預防措施，才能有效防範傷害、職業病與成本的損失，所以工地管理者必須充分了解風險管控的機制與落實執行。意謂優質團隊的每位成員都要有基本的四大正念。

(一) 尊重生命的信念　　　　(二) 恪遵法令的概念

(三) 全員共識的理念　　　　(四) 風險控制的觀念

圖 8　優質團隊落實全員安衛的意象圖

Figure 8. Diagram of total safety & health with fulfill by excellence quality team

第四章　工程風險管理 Risk Management of Construction

4-1 安全與危險的區別 Distinction between safety & danger.

4-2 本質安全的重要性 Importance of intrinsic safety.

4-3 解析施工風險評估作業（蓮藕現象）Analyzing operation of risk assessment of construction (Phenomenon of Lotus Root).

4-4 意外災害暨緊急應變 Disaster occurred with emergency response.

4-5 工地全方位緊急救援演練 Drill of emergency rescue in comprehensive at site.

4-1 安全與危險的區別 Distinction between safety & danger

　　對工程而言，安全與危險可謂一體兩面的體現，設計階段設計者就設計的理念，鮮少去考量施工的安全性，大部分總承攬商鑑於成本及利潤的考量，現場的設施及設備安全，除非有預算的編列，通常十之八九的營造業者均把持著符合職業安全衛生法暨相關法規的最低標準規定即可。試問工地管理者，這樣的管理作法工地安全嗎？

　　所謂安全，它的意義，就是工地不論何時、何地，管理者所做的任何事（進度／安全／品質）都要有正確的決定，防止災害的發生。

　　（What safety is ..., Whatever one thing as progress rate、safety、quality, site manager should do that really mattered was to get this right to prevent the accident happen.）

　　綜合而言，工地落實優質管理機制首重強調安全優先的重要性，工地安全性自然提高，相反地，危險的作業環境則自然減少。

圖 9　工地優質管理機制安全與危險走勢圖

Figure 9. Trend diagram of safety & danger witch was excellence quality management at work site.

4-2 本質安全的重要性 Importance of intrinsic safety

　　營建業從基礎開挖直到竣工交屋，可謂百工的行業，雖然各分項工程可言術業有專攻，但工地管理者也必須於作業前經由溝通方式，強調分項作業本質安全的重要性。藉由管理者與施工者的充分解析，可分成兩大補強事項如下說明，以彌補落實本質安全不足之處。

圖 10　什麼是本質安全？

Figure 10. What is intrinsic safety?

一、工程管理人員應落實的關鍵作業 Crucial operation should be fulfilled with supervisor /manager

(一) 進場作業人員應遵行的事項

1. 完成營建業進場 6 小時一般安全衛生教育訓練。
2. 接受管理人員於作業前潛在危害因子的告知及注意事項。
3. 作業主管應在現場監督及協調作業相關事項。
4. 作業人員應於作業前穿戴完整的個人防護具。
5. 作業人員應遵照安全標準作業流程施工，防止事故發生。
6. 工作者本身職能不足（包括：法規、危害、技能、行為認知及態度），應給予再教育訓練。

(二) 工程管理人員應執行的事項

1. 每日晨間定時召集工具箱交談，明確說明 5W/1H 的運用。
2. 現場臨時設施要張掛明顯的標示及警告標誌。
3. 增加作業區安全衛生巡檢的頻率，使作業勞工及設施符合規定。
4. 每日定時開會檢討安全衛生巡檢的缺失，並研商改善對策。
5. 下工前落實清潔整理 5S 機制，使作業區再轉向成安全作業場所。
6. 現場設施設備未妥善規劃或有缺失，管理措施不當也需檢討改進。
7. 每月安全衛生協議組織會議針對現場缺失的分析圖表（如下圖示），告知所有的協議組織會員，必須加強及改進現場的安全防護作業。

表 3　分項作業各類缺失比較表

Chart3. Chart of comparison for various deficiencies with sectors work.

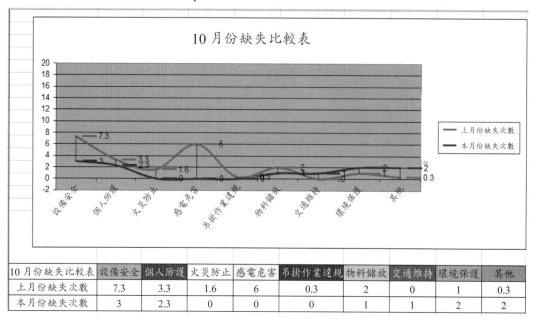

10月份缺失比較表	設備安全	個人防護	火災防止	感電危害	吊掛作業違規	物料儲放	交通維持	環境保護	其他
上月份缺失次數	7.3	3.3	1.6	6	0.3	2	0	1	0.3
本月份缺失次數	3	2.3	0	0	0	1	1	2	2

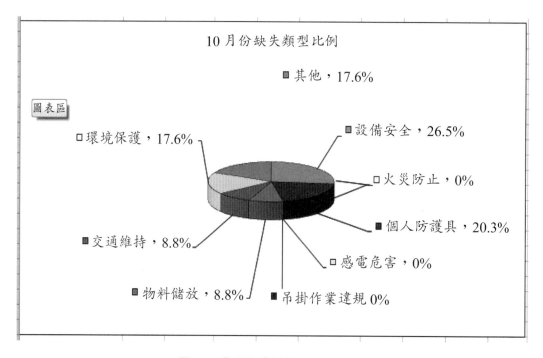

圖 11　分項作業缺失類型比例圖

Figure 11. Diagram of scale was with deficiencies of sector works.

4-3 解析施工風險評估作業（蓮藕現象）Analyzing operation of risk assessment of construction (Phenomenon of Lotus Root)

一、分項工程作業評估的關鍵步驟 Crucial procedure of assessment for sector works.

(一) 危害辨識 Hazard identification

作業前針對施工流程的危害因子，包括場所、作業環境、天候狀況、其他等。

(二) 風險分析 Risk analysis

媒介物、不安全設備、不安全行為、其他等。

(三) 風險評量 Risk assessment

針對（嚴重度／可能性）其加乘數值大小做分析。研判現場作業區的防護設施及設備是否符合安全相關規範要求，表示風險是可接受的。如未能達標，表示風險是不可接受的，工地管理者必需提出對策進行改善。

(四) 風險對策 Risk strategy

考量現場狀況使用 5W/1H（人、事、時、地、物／方法）及消除風險、降低風險、工程控制、管理控制、個人防護具等措施。

二、危害辨識的目的 Purpose of hazard identification

工作場所環境現況及工程作業內容，依工程師的專業知識並參酌過去災害案例，以辨識潛存於工作場所及作業過程中之危害。

作業前的危害辨識要因分析

〈蓮藕現象〉　　　　　　　　　　(1) 危害辨識

分項工程拆解圖　　　　　　　　　　＊關鍵作業＊
　　　　　　　　　　　　　　　1. 工作場所相關環境危害。
　　　　　　　　　　　　　　　2. 工程安全本質危害。
　　　　　　　　　　　　　　　3. 營建機械設備危害。
　　　　　　　　　　　　　　　4. 危險物質材料危害。
　　　　　　　　　　　　　　　5. 天候異常及天災災害。

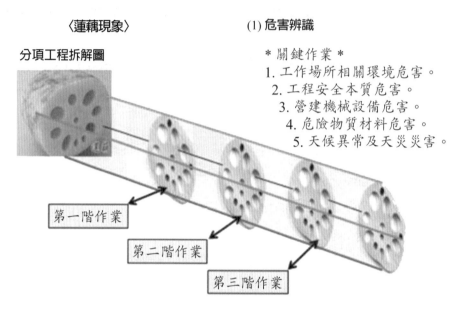

第一階作業

第二階作業

第三階作業

圖 12　分項工程作業拆解階梯圖

Figure 12. Diagram of segmented was step of sector works.

〈蓮藕現象〉　　　　　　　　(2) 風險肇因

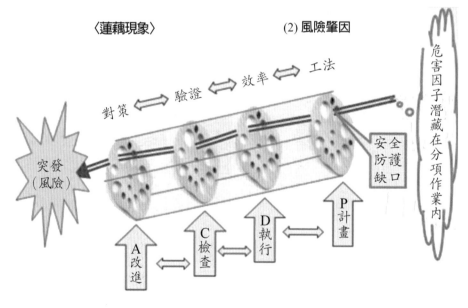

圖 13　危害與風險關係圖

Figure 13. Related diagram was in hazard & risk.

三、風險分析的目的 Purpose of risk analysis

工程分項作業進程中，分析的目的是要找出致災要因亦潛藏在各階段拆解作業中的危害因子及媒介物、不安全設備、不安全行為、其他等。

經由 P > D > C > A 的優質管理機制，研議有效對策，於作業中做好符合安全規定的防護設施，防止意外事故的發生。

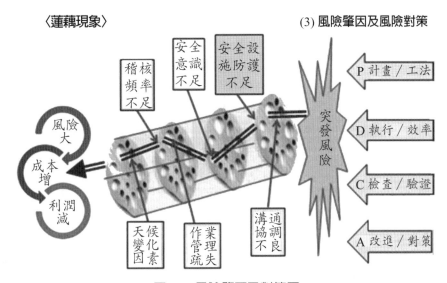

圖 14　風險肇因及對策圖

Figure 14. Diagram was of risk which cause, effect & strategy.

四、風險評量作業 Operation of risk assessment.

風險評量的關鍵作業 Crucial operations of risk assessment.

開工前需分析本工程各分項作業進行中、可預期發生之**高風險危害作業**，例如：

a. 高架作業（**墜落事故**），

b. 電氣作業（**感電事故**），

c. 支撐作業（**倒塌事故**），

d. 動火作業（**火災事故**），

e. 侷限空間作業（**缺氧事故**）等。

以及作業進行中各類缺失的比較及缺失間比例的高低和無法預期的意外事故，均是我們評量的重要項目，進而研擬相關對策，防止可能的災害發生。工地管理者可以運用參照風險評量作業表單及風險矩陣表單來管控風險和研擬對策降低風險，以降低人員及財產的損失。

公司名稱	部門	評估日期	評估人員	審核者		
營造股份有限公司		108.03.01				

1.作業/流程名稱	2.危害辨識及後果（危害可能造成後果之情境描述）	3.現有防護設施	4. 評估風險			5.降低風險所採取之控制措施	6. 控制後預估風險		
			嚴重度	可能性	風險等級		嚴重度	可能性	風險等級
施工架工程/吊運工程/人員	人員於吊掛作業中無相關掛服被開例罰單	入場前操作手及吊掛手證書（照）資料確認	S2 (P2)	P3 (S3)		1.每日作業危害告知。2.作業時確實巡視、督導，若有違反，停止作業至違規事項消除後得復工。	S2 (P2)	P1 (S1)	

圖 15　營建工程風險評量作業所使用的標準版格式

Figure 15. Standard from of risk assessment was used for construction project.

風險矩陣 Risk Matrix		可能性等級 Probability			
		P4	P3	P2	P1
嚴重度等級 Severity	S4	16	12	8	4
	S3	12	9	6	3
	S2	8	6	4	2
	S1	4	3	2	1

16—高度危急風險	立即停工改善
12～8—危險風險	立即改善
6～3—高度風險	改善時間一日
2—中度風險	改善時間二日
1—低度風險	改善時間三日

圖 16　風險矩陣分析的嚴重度等級及可能性等級包含處理對策

Figure 16. Diagram of risk matrix included the grades of severity & probability with strategy.

五、風險對策 Risk strategy

　　風險對策的目的是利用有效的推論配合設計者及工程人員的專業知識和實務經驗，考量現場狀況及預知施工期間天氣變化的掌握，進行作業人員有效率的調派，發揮全方位的效能。使用 5W/1H（人、事、時、地、物／方法）及消除風險、降低風險、工程控制、管理控制、個人防護具等管理機制，經由公司的決策者同意執行，達到預測的殘餘風險是可以管控的，亦減少公司成本增加及利潤減少的情況發生。

圖 17　決策者開會討論風險對策的樣態

Figure 17. Meeting of risk strategy was made decision by steering commisio

4-4 意外災害暨緊急應變 Disaster occurred with emergency response

　　「意外災害」是指突然、意外發生需立刻處理的事件，營建工程施工作業期間會遇到的緊急事件。可能包括天然災害（颱風、地震、水災）、火災、爆炸、危害或人員墜落、缺氧、感電、交通事故、暴力事件、外傷出血、停斷電等事故或災害造成勞工受到災害，亦職業災害，即勞工就業場所之建築物、設備、原料、材料、化學物品、氣體、蒸氣、粉塵等，或作業活動引起之勞工疾病、傷害、殘廢或死亡等。

　　工地範圍發生任何職災均會造成工地人員受傷及設施財物的損失，任何突發情況發生時，工地安全衛生部門應立即啟動緊急應變機制及救援小組成立，進行人員的救助、災害現場的掌控及救援作業的展開。工地範圍發生職災，都是有跡可循，縱然工地自主管理非常落實，所謂作業環境在百密一疏的情況下，造成職災發生是可以預料的，唯有落實職災的事故調查，找尋出正確的原因及正確的防制對策，才能將意外災害澈底消弭。

一、職業災害發生的潛變要因 Potential factors of occupation disaster

(一) 安全顧慮 Safety concern

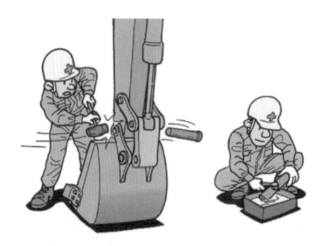

圖 18　顯示狀況可能會造成作業人員的傷害，財務損失肇因作業環境呈現不安全隱患存在。

Figure 18. Showed dangerous condition where caused the worker injury or lose belongings.

(二) 虛驚事件 Near miss

圖 19　顯示狀況千鈞一髮，指非預期的虛驚事件即將發生，潛在危害是人為因素所造成的，並且造成安全作業的困擾。

Figure 19. Showed dangerous condition which uncorrected operation by worker that operator made the procedure in persecution.

(三) 意外事故 Incident

圖 20　顯示狀況指突發的事故，將造成人員的輕傷或財產損失，但事故發生的紀錄值得管理者留存參考。

Figure 20. Showed dangerous condition which sudden occurrence to make the worker got minor injuries which record could keep in file & reference.

(四) 職業災害 Occupation disaster include accident & fatal

　　依照職業安全衛生法規定，構成職業災害的條件如下列所述：

1. 發生死亡災害。
2. 發生災害之罹災人數在三人以上。
3. 發生災害之罹災人數在一人以上，且需住院治療。
4. 其他經中央主管機關指定公告之災害

圖 21　顯示狀況工作場所疏於安全防護對策而發生墜落災害

Figure 21. Showed dangerous condition where did not has safety protection to made worker fall down at site.

(五) 災害潛變進階關係與斷鏈對策 Update route of potential creeping & strategy of chain broken to Accident

圖 22 職業災害發生的進階要因圖

Figure 22. Major factor was update route to cause accident.

圖 23 防止災害進階發生的斷鏈對策

Figure 23. Strategy of prevent the Accident which was the route of broken chain.

(六)工地意外災害緊急應變流程 Flow chart of emergency response as accident occurred at site

表 4 緊急應變通報流程表

Chart4. Flow chart of emergency response

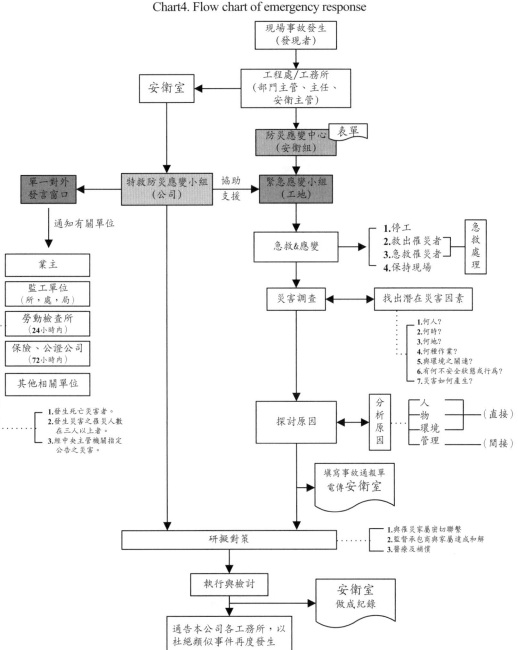

(七) 急救處理步驟 Sequence of first aid

1. 創傷急救：止血、防止汙染、送醫。
2. 骨折急救：固定傷肢、送醫。
3. 燒燙傷急救：沖、脫、泡、蓋、送。

(八) 口對口人工呼吸法實施要領 Essential of artificial respiration with mouth to mouth

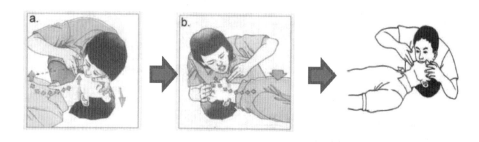

圖 24　口對口人工呼吸法關鍵三步驟

Figure 24 . Crucial 3 steps of artificial respiration with mouth to mouth.

1. 使病患仰臥，用手指摳出患者嘴裡異物，托起頸部，讓頭部微向後仰，下顎凸起，並解開其衣領及皮帶。
2. 把病患之下巴向上扳起。
3. 捏住病患鼻孔，緊貼病患張開之嘴巴用力吹氣（成人每分鐘十五次），並注意其胸部有無鼓起。
4. 把嘴移開使病患吐氣，數二後重複吹氣，直至病患被救活為止。

(九) 心肺復甦術實施要領 Essential operation of CPR-Cardio Pulmonary Resuscitation

圖 25　心肺復甦術關鍵三要點

Figure 25. Crucial points in 3 of cardiopulmonary resuscitation.

1. 檢查呼吸道、頸動脈確定有無呼吸及心跳。
2. 若只無呼吸立即進行人工呼吸。
3. 若無呼吸及心跳，立即進行心肺復甦術配合人工呼吸及胸外按摩（一人施救時，壓縮心臟十五下、人工呼吸二下，重複四次後檢查呼吸、脈搏，若仍無呼吸及心跳時，重複上述動作；二人施行時壓縮心臟五下、人工呼吸一下）。

(十) 自動體外電擊去顫器 AED Automated External Defibrillator

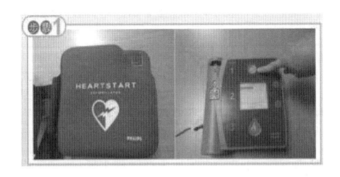

使用步驟如下：
步驟一：打開電源開關。語音指示系統將啟動，聽指示進行以下步驟。
步驟二：貼上電擊片，插入導線。右側電擊片置於胸骨右上緣，鎖骨下方；左側電擊片置於左乳頭外側，其上緣距離左腋窩下約 7 公分。
步驟三：自動分析心律。
步驟四：確定無人接觸病患，依機器指示電擊。

(十一) 救護車接送傷者到醫院 Victim was delivered to hospital for therapy

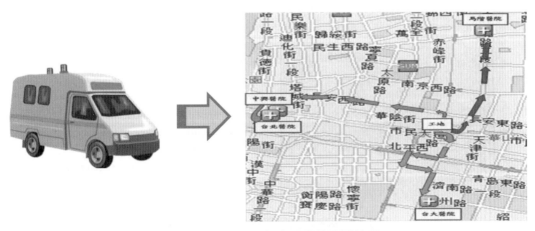

圖 26　緊急救援受傷者醫療後送路線圖

Figure 26. Route of emergency deliveried injury to hospital for medical therapy.

表 5　政府機關及救援單位緊急聯絡電話表

Chart5. Emergency contact telephone table of rescue unit & authority of government

	醫院名稱	地址	電話
醫療體系	臺大醫院	臺北市中山南路 7 號	2312-3456
	臺北醫院	臺北市中正區鄭州路 40 號	2581-0429
	中興醫院	臺北市中正區鄭州路 145 號	2521-3234
	馬偕醫院	臺北市中山區中山北路二段 92 號	2543-3535

	消防單位	地址	電話
消防體系	火警台		119
	建成消防分隊	臺北市大同區承德路二段 25 號	2559-3748
	華山消防隊	臺北市中正區北平東路 1 號	2341-2668
	城中消防隊	臺北市重慶南路一段 1 號	2381-2839
	延平消防分隊	臺北市延平北路一段 88 號	2558-2105

4-5 工地全方位緊急救援演練 Drill of emergency rescue in comprehensive at site

一、兵棋推演 Table-top exercise

➢ 兵棋推演 Table-top exercise

主要目的：所有不同救援小組經由位置的安排，利用口頭演練虛擬的腳本，其目的在於熟悉各單位協調聯繫呈報的機制，使搶救急救的任務能即時完成，並達到預期的目標。

Major Purpose:

Members in different characters of rescue teams as assigned mission are arranged to sit around the table to practice the scenario which major purpose makes rescuer who realize the emergency contact system to good for the rescue work which be completed in time & meet the work be completed in time & meet the goal as expected.

圖 27　每年度定期舉行兵棋推演的態樣

Figure 27. Table-top exercise should be held in regularly of annual.

二、實兵演練 Mock-up drill

➤ 實兵演練 Mock-up drill

主要目的：救援組別任務雖然不同，經由演練中熟悉協調聯繫的機制，建立各組間合作的默契，進而發揮團隊的最大效率。

Major Purpose：
The rescue teams are
Assigned in difierent
mission for the Mock-
Up Drill that everyone
can realize the co-ordination
system when drill in operation.
To establish the agree of
implicated to develop the
great efficient of teams.

圖 28　每年度參加緊急救援實兵演練比賽的態樣

Figure 28. Participated the Mock-up drill 0f emergency rescue in annual.

三、防汛沙包疊砌演練 Exercise of sand bags to pile up.

➤ 防汛沙包疊砌演練
Exercise of Sand Bag Pile for Flood Prevention

圖 29　每年防汛期前自行舉辦沙包疊砌訓練

Figure 29. Annual training of sandbags pile up to prevent the flood.

(一) 沙包防汛使用方法

1. 金字塔形式沙包防汛，主要是通過一層一層地堆疊（根據汛情嚴重程度，有時還要多疊幾排），抵擋水的沖擊力。這個原理應用在沙包擺放時，就是沙包科學擺放方式，可以選用梯形擺放。因為「沙包牆」下部受力比較大，上部受力比較小，這種擺放方式可以在抵抗洪水時起到事半功倍的作用。

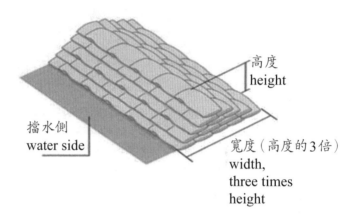

高度
height

擋水側
water side

寬度（高度的3倍）
width,
three times
height

2. **磚牆形式**就是下面這種疊放方式，第二層的沙包要放在第一層兩個沙包中間，這樣才能有效擋水。

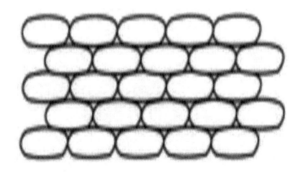

3. **人字形式**就是將每個沙包依序以相鄰兩者重疊的方式交疊過去。若第一層從右邊疊起，第二層則從左邊疊回。技巧說明如下：

   (1) 沙包口不一定紮上，堆疊前可以先將袋口往下摺，壓在沙包下，袋口朝向水流的方向，避免沙包被沖開。

   (2) 每擺好一個沙包，就用腳踩一踩，讓鬆軟的沙質更為緊密，可有效防水。

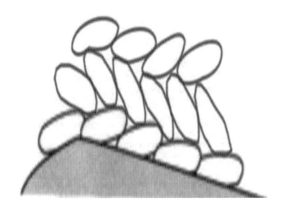

四、防火消防演練 Exercise the fire fightting

圖 30　每年度自行舉辦防火消防演練態樣

Figure 30. Opening emergency response with fire fight exercise.

圖 31　每年度自行舉辦防火演練參與者使用乾粉滅火器滅火態樣

Figure 31. Participators carried the dry extinguisher to practiced the fire fight.

五、滅火器的口訣 Rhyme for remembering of fire extinguisher

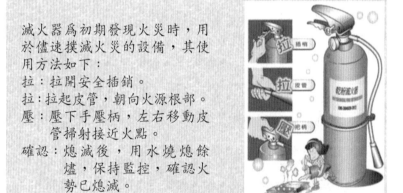

滅火器為初期發現火災時，用於儘速撲滅火災的設備，其使用方法如下：

拉：拉開安全插銷。

拉：拉起皮管，朝向火源根部。

壓：壓下手壓柄，左右移動皮管掃射接近火點。

確認：熄滅後，用水燒熄餘燼，保持監控，確認火勢已熄滅。

圖 32　乾粉滅火器

Figure 32. Dry powered fire extinguishers

第五章 工地高風險作業的管理防制及對策 Crucial Controlling & Strategy Were to The High Risk Operation at Work Site

5-1 何謂職業災害 What occupational disaster is?

5-2 墜落防止 Fall prevention.

5-3 感電災害防制 Accident of electric shock prevention.

5-4 倒塌崩塌防制的關鍵要領 Crucial skill of prevention for collapse & tumble down.

5-5 火災防制的關鍵要領 Crucial skill of prevention for fire accident.

5-6 缺氧作業的關鍵要領 Crucial skill of work for hyposia operation.

5-7 營建工地熱危害的預防與對策 Precaution & strategy of heat hazard at construction site.

5-1 何謂職業災害 What occupational disaster is?

　　職業安全衛生法第 2 條規定，職業災害係指勞動場所之建築物、機械、設備、原料、材料、化學品、氣體、蒸氣、粉塵等，或作業活動及其他職業上原因引起之工作者疾病、傷害、失能或死亡。

圖 33　工地發生職災態樣

Figure 33. Forms of occupational disasters at work site.

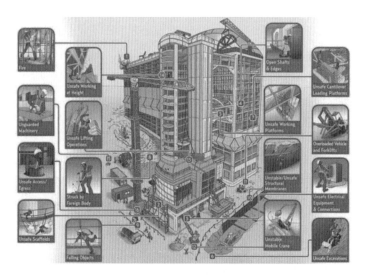

圖 34　工地各類型職災圖示

Figure 34. Appearance of occupational disasters at work site.

職業災害類型 Types of occupational disaster.

(一) 墜落

指人從樹木、建築物、施工架、機械、搭乘物、階梯、斜面等落下情形（不含交通事故）。

(二) 感電

指接觸帶電體或因通電而人體受衝擊之情況。

(三) 物體倒塌

指堆積物（包括內含）、施工架、建築物等倒塌碰觸到人造成傷亡之情形。

(四) 火災

指以危險物本身為媒介物產生之火災；又危險物以外之情形，則為以火源媒介物產生之火災。

(五) 缺氧

一般正常空氣中氧氣濃度約 21%，如果在 18% 以下作業有可能產生身體不適，在 16% 以下會造成人腦判斷力降低而易產生不安全行為，所以將氧氣濃度低於 18% 以下稱為缺氧危險作業。

(六) 跌倒

指人在同一平面倒下，絆跤或滑倒之情形（含車輛機械等跌倒，不含交通事故）。

(七) 衝撞

指除去墜落、滾落、跌倒外，以人為主體碰觸到靜止物或動態吊物、機械之部分等打到人及飛落之情形（含與車輛機械衝撞，不含交通事故）。

(八) 物體飛落

指以飛行物、落下物為主體碰觸到人之情形（含研削物破裂、切斷片、切削粉飛來及自持物落下之情形；又容器破裂應分類為物體破裂）。

(九) 爆炸

指壓力之急激發生或開放之結果，帶有爆音引起膨脹之情況而言。破裂除外，包含水蒸氣爆炸，在容器、裝置內部爆炸之情況。容器、裝置等本身破裂時，亦歸屬於本類。

(十) 被撞

指除物體飛落、物體倒崩、崩塌外，以物為主體碰觸到人之情形。

(十一) 被切、割、擦傷

指被擦傷的情況，及以被擦傷的狀態而被切割等之情況。

(十二) 被夾、被捲

指人在被夾、被捲狀態壓扭等情形。

(十三) 溺斃

指墜落水中致死之情形。

(十四) 與高溫、低溫之接觸

指與高溫、低溫之接觸，包含暴露於高溫或低溫環境下之情況。

(十五) 鐵公路交通事故

指因火車、汽(機)車等交通工具所發生之事故。

5-2 墜落防止 Fall prevention.

一、職災防止作業的關鍵要領 Crucial essential operation of occupation disaster prevention.

(一) 墜落危害防止，注意本質安全及作業前危害辨識。

(二) 墜落防止嚴格要求作業人員穿戴完全個人防護具。

(三) 地面作業、護欄、護蓋、安全帶、安全網、控制通行區、警示線安全監控系統（警告措施）等方法，依序考量防止墜落職災發生。

(四) 創新作業方法使勞工於地面完成作業，以減少高處作業的墜落風險。

二、墜落防止對策的優質圖片 Excellence images as strategy of prevent fall accident.

圖 35　墜落意外示意圖

Figure 35. Schematic diagram of fall accident

【A 字梯使用方式】

圖 36　鋁合梯（A 字梯）使用的標準方式

Figure 36. Standard ways of aluminum step ladder twin using.

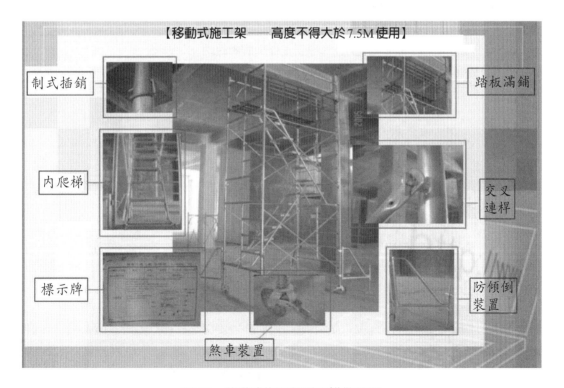

圖 37　移動式施工架重要構件說明

Figure 37. Illustration was major components of mobile scaffold.

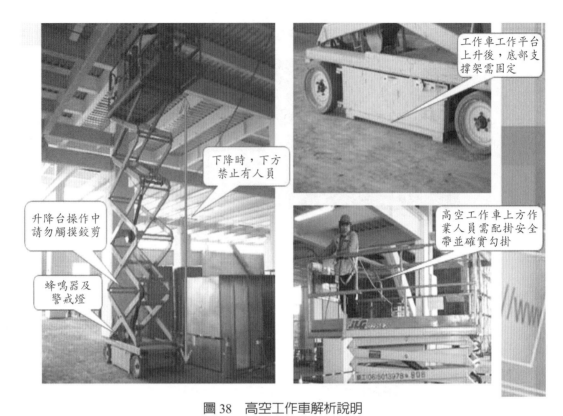

工作車工作平台上升後，底部支撐架需固定

下降時，下方禁止有人員

升降台操作中請勿觸摸鉸剪

蜂鳴器及警戒燈

高空工作車上方作業人員需配掛安全帶並確實勾掛

圖 38　高空工作車解析說明

Figure 38. Illustration of analyzing was to aerial work platform.

作業高度超過 20M 以上應使用移動式起重機及直結式吊籃（吊籃應有載重結構計算書及人員穿戴背負式安全帶）

圖 39　移動式起重機加掛吊籃解析說明

Figure 39. Illustration was a bucket which mounted on the mobile crane.

圖 40　連續壁抓掘作業導溝防墜安全措施

Figure 40. Fall prevention protection of guide ditch in diaphragm wall operation.

圖 41　開挖作業時安全護欄可拆除改用交通錐防護

Figure 41. Using the traffic cone substitute the guard rail during the excavation progressing.

圖 42　水平支撐人行動線需裝置安全母索

Figure 42. Generatrix of strutting should install the life line.

圖 43　水平支撐的覆工鈑開口需裝置安全護欄

Figure 43. Open space of checked steel cover desk onto strutting should erect the guardrail.

圖 44　水平支撐的覆工鈑下方需張掛安全防墜網

Figure 44. Safety nets of fall prevention should hang up below the checked steel cover desks.

圖 45　水平支撐開口依規定設置安全護欄及腳趾板

Figure 45. Safety guard rails with toe boards should erected on the checked metro desks.

圖 46　覆工鈑上方需規劃安全通道以防止材料亂置有飛落之虞

Figure 46. Planned safety path on the steel cover decks for material deposited to prevent falling incident occurred.

圖 47　水平支撐上方需規劃設置人員安全通道及安全護欄

Figure 47. Planned & erected as safety aisle of workers on the strutting.

圖 48　連續壁與水平支撐界臨的安全通道需設置安全護欄

Figure 48. Safety guard rail erected on the path onto strutting adjacent diaphragm wall.

圖 49 施工架組裝配合上下設施的安全作業平台

Figure 49. Scaffold assembled with ladders for safety working platforms.

圖 50 框式施工架組立時必須依法設置安全防墜網

Figure 50. Safety nets should spread & tire on the proper height of scaffold which assembled as frame type.

圖 51　樓層間樓梯模板進行作業必須設置臨時防墜護欄

Figure 51. Form works in progressing of stair way between floor should erect the guard rail to prevent fall.

圖 52　樓層電梯豎井的開口位置必須張掛防墜安全網

Figure 52. Safety net as fall prevent should spread & tie on the rebar which around the elevator shaft.

圖 53　電梯豎井於模板作業前必須張掛防墜的安全網

Figure 53. Safety net as fall prevent should spread & tie on the elevator shaft prior form work in progress.

圖 54　樓梯間混凝土澆注完成應設置安全護欄

Figure 54. Guard rail should erect on the stair way when concrete pumping finished.

圖 55 樓地板的開口除了張掛防墜網，還要設置安全護欄。

Figure 55. Safety nets should spread & tie with guardrail on the pit of the floor.

圖 56 筏基開口防蚊及防墜的安全措施

Figure 56. Safety measures of anti-mosquitoes & fall prevention to the pit of raft foundation.

圖 57　筏基開口完全覆蓋的防墜措施

Figure 57. Pits of raft foundation where has been coved completely to prevent fall accident.

圖 58　筏基開口完全覆蓋及明顯的警告標示

Figure 58. Pit of raft foundation where has been coved with warning mark.

圖 59　電梯豎井需設置安全柵欄及警告標示

Figure 59. Safety fences with warning notice should erect at lift vertical shaft.

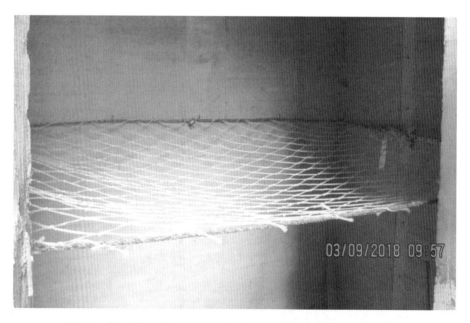

圖 60　各樓層電梯豎井內的防墜網不得移除直到結構體完工

Figure 60. Safety net should not remove of hoist way until the pump work has completed of construction.

圖 61 利用電梯豎井吊運泥作材料要事先申請同意及完備的個人防護具

Figure 61. The pemission was gotten of hoisting operation at hoist way with completely PPE for hoist materials of masonry work

圖 62 室內牆壁粉刷作業使用有護欄的作業平台

Figure 62. Prepared the platform with guardrail for the plaster work of wall

圖 63　粉刷作業使用安全的設施無墜落之虞

Figure 63. Prepared the safety facility for plaster work to prevent the fall factor

圖 64　樓梯間進行泥作粉刷時，採用防墜網替代安全護欄。

Figure 64. Safety net had been substituted for guard rail when staircase in progressing of mason work.

圖 65　施工架組裝作業人員必須穿戴背負式安全帶

Figure 65.Worker should wear the full body harness with lanyard of one large snap hook.

圖 66　作業人員於施工架上作業也必須配戴使用腰掛式安全帶

Figure 66. Workers have worn the waist safey belt when they work on the scaffold.

圖67　施工架組裝完成後，與結構體的間隙為防止人員墜落，每一層施工架需張掛長條防墜網。

Figure 67. Gap between structure and scaffold where should spread & tie the safety net with layer by layer to prevent the fall accident occurred.

施工架延伸配件──三角架及輔助板料

圖 68　施工架組裝完成後，與結構體的間隙為防止人員墜落，可跳層施作延伸平台。

Figure 68. Gap between structure and scaffold where should mount the extend platform with tripod of layer jump to prevent the fall accident occurred.

施工架組裝標準照片——內外側交叉拉桿、下拉桿及腳趾板
等（如施工架每層外側有張掛護網，其腳趾板可以選擇不做）

圖 69　施工架標準構件組裝完成後，如有拆除則需復歸完全，以防止墜落意外發生。

Figure 69. Typical scaffold which components were disassemblied for work then should rehabilitate until work is completed.

圖 70　施工架組裝的安全步道均需安裝安全護欄

Figure 70. Safety path onto top layer should mount the guard rail on both sides.

圖 71　施工架組裝均採扶手先行工法，以防止人員墜落。

Figure 71. To prevent fall accident that carry out the method of guard rail in priority during scaffold in assembling.

圖 72　鋼骨結構配合固定式起重機（塔吊）作業的態樣

Figure 72. Tower crane mounted to steel structure construction in operation.

圖 73　鋼構作業主管作業前，檢查作業人員個人防護具及作業檢點的重要性。

Figure 73. Superior examines the PPE of steel workers & giving the notice of checking the facilities & tools are important prior work starting.

圖 74　鋼樑必須安裝垂直桿柱及安全母索，以利作業人員勾掛使用。

Figure 74. Vertical rod should be mounted with safety lanyard on the H beam for workers hook up.

圖 75　鋼樑吊掛組裝時，作業人員勾掛使用安全母索以防止墜落發生。

Figure 75. Steel workers used the large snap hook on the lanyard of harness to prevent the fall accident on the connection work.

圖 76　鋼構作業人員使用背負式安全帶雙勾掛確保作業安全

Figure 76. Steel workers using two large snap hooker of full body harness that hook on the lanyard to keep the worker in safety.

圖 77　鋼構電焊作業人員使用叉架（簡易式坐板），其下方必須有安全防墜網張掛。

Figure 77. Steel welder used the fork shelf with C buckle as simplification plat for welding work where below that safety nets should spread & tighten.

圖 78　鋼構作業人員使用安全工作架時，必須使用勾掛安全帶。

Figure 78. Steel workers used the safety bucket to weld the connection of beam & column that they should use large snap hooker to life line.

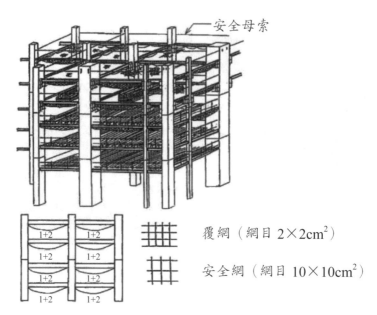

覆網（網目 $2 \times 2cm^2$）

安全網（網目 $10 \times 10cm^2$）

圖 79 鋼構作業為防止墜落事故發生，張掛水平式覆網（網目 $2 \times 2cm^2$）加安全網（網目 $10 \times 10cm^2$）需平整完全。

Figure 79. For prevented the fall accident that horizontal open space of steel frame should spread the safety net in overlying which include two different sizes of net mesh as one size is $4cm^2$ with other size is $100cm^2$.

圖 80 鋼構作業為防止人員墜落意外，可於外側鋼樑加掛垂直半幕式防墜網。

Figure 80. Prevent the fall accident that one way was to hang up the verticle half shield of safety net onto the out side of beam.

圖 81　鋼構作業為防止墜落事件，可於鋼結構外側加掛全幕式防墜網。

Figure 81. All shield of safety net which had been wrapped up all the steel structure to prevent works to caused the fall accident.

圖 82　鋼結構吊掛組裝作業高度超過 20M 的情況下，也可使用搭乘設備（吊籃）。

Figure 82. Cage hoist was used to connect the work of beam & column where working of steel structure should more than over 20 meters height.

起重機吊掛搭乘設備搭載或吊升人員作業注意事項（民國 98 年 10 月 12 日修正）

使用固定式起重機或移動式起重機從事貨櫃裝卸、船舶維修、高煙囪施工等尚無其他安全作業替代方法，或臨時性、小規模、短時間、作業性質特殊，經採取防止墜落等措施者。但除使用移動式起重機於道路或鄰樓道路從事作業者外，從事垂直高度二十公尺以下之高處作業，仍不得使用搭乘設備搭載或吊升人員作業。

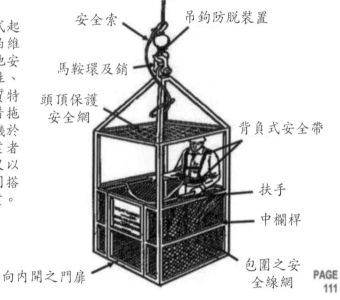

圖 83　鋼結構作業有關人員搭乘設備（吊籃）的相關法令施行細則

Figure 83. According the subsidiary regulation of riding the cage hoist for steel structure connection works.

圖 84　鋼結構作業符合安全的搭乘設備（吊籃）均有簽認合格標示編號

Figure 84. Cage hoist was recognized & approved by authority that issued the approved series of number as upper right image.

5-3 感電災害防制 Accident of lectric shock prevention

感電災害原因就如其他職業災害一樣，不外乎是不安全的動作和不安全的設備（環境）所引起的，然而這些引隱患都可藉由良好的電氣安全設施、適當的電氣安全教育訓練、健全的安全衛生管理組織（人員）及嚴格的管理監督與自動檢查來排除危害因子的存在。防止感電之最好方式為使電氣設備不漏電，人體觸摸不到帶電體，其次為加強各種安全保護裝置和措施，實施自動檢查與訂定安全衛生工作守則，加強電氣安全教育訓練與設置安全衛生組織（人員）及急救處理等。而就感電職災之防止技術，則可概分為下列九種方式：

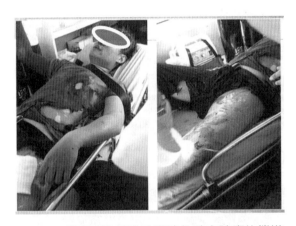

圖 85　感電罹災者後送醫院急診室診療的態樣

Figure 85. Victim of electric shock was delivered to the emergency room of hospital for therapy.

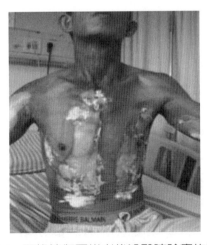

圖 86　閃烙燒傷罹災者後送醫院診療的態樣

Figure 86. Victim of burn of electric arc flash was delivered to the hospital for therapy.

一、感電防制作業的關鍵要領 Crucial essential operation of electric shock prevention

圖 87　分電盤不得隨意開啟，以防止人員發生感電意外。

Figure 87. Distribution panel box should be closed to prevent the workers in electric shock.

(一) **隔離**：隔離乃使帶電的電氣設備或線路與工作者分開或保持距離，使勞工不易碰觸。

(二) **絕緣**：絕緣為保持或加強電氣線路及設備之良好電氣絕緣狀態，接近架空高壓裸電線作業時，於高壓線上加裝防護線管等。

(三) **雙重絕緣**：雙重絕緣即強化電氣設備之絕緣。在一般電氣設備上，其帶電部分與金屬製外箱（殼）間必有絕緣。

(四) **防護器具**：防護器具乃作業者穿戴電氣絕緣用防護具，或使用活線作業用器具及裝備。譬如：穿戴絕緣手套、絕緣鞋、安全帽等；使用絕緣棒、絕緣工具及絕緣作業用工程車等。

(五) **接地**：接地係將電氣設備的金屬製外箱（殼）等目的物以導體與大地做良好的電氣性連接，保持目的物與大地同電位（這也是一般最常見的感電防止方法）。

(六) **低電壓**：使用低電壓為本質安全用電方式之一，在某些特殊場所，如在壓力容器內從事檢修工作時，由於其導電性良好且作業時人體易汗溼，因此其使用電壓必須限制在安全電壓範圍內，以防觸電時發生感電災害。

(七) **安全保護裝置**：安全保護裝置泛指一切施加於電路或設備上之保安裝置，其目的主要在於發生漏電時，能自動偵測出漏電而啟斷電路或發出警報訊號。包括：一般常見之漏電斷路器、漏電警報器。

(八) **非接地系統**：非接地系統乃指供電的電源系統（一次側）為一非接地之供電系統，其
一般作法是於接地之低壓電源系統中，再以一具隔離變壓器將該電源系統轉成負載系
統（二次側）為非接地電源系統，以供電給負載使用。

二、閃烙燒傷發生的原因 Cause of burn & arc flush

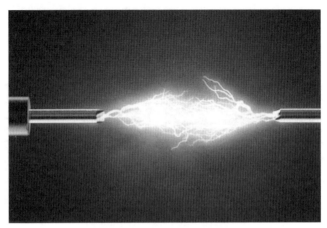

圖 88　閃烙現象示意圖
Figure 88. Schematic diagram was appearance of arc flush.

　　工地電弧閃光造成的傷害很多，就人員的傷害來說，包括視力或聽力的損害、燒傷、
灼傷，嚴重的話甚至需要進行皮膚移植與復健，再更嚴重的話，可能會導致死亡。電弧閃
烙短路的導因，主要可以分成兩個部分；

　　第一個部分：為外部的物體侵入，包括昆蟲、灰塵汙染或溼氣結露滲透等；或者人為
疏失，如工具不小心觸碰到電源，導致與電源接觸和不恰當的工作程序等。

　　第二個部分：為設備故障，例如缺乏定期維護保養，導致設備或導電體絕緣劣化破
壞，此外，過電壓、過電流與過載等原因也會造成設備故障。

三、閃烙燒傷防制作業的關鍵要領 Crucial essential operation of burn
arc flush prevention

(一) 安全計畫內容說明標準作業程序及明確責任。

(二) 閃烙危害程度的計算及重新調整爆炸的能量破壞。

(三) 指出及防制缺失發生，提供標準的個人防護具給工作人員穿戴。

(四) 維修工具必須符合工作安全的規定，亦可採用遠端遙控作業。

(五) 設備上必須有警告標示，顯示危害分析，警示縮短清潔時間。

四、工地防制感電對策的優質圖片 Excellence images as strategy of electric shock prevention at work site

圖 89　甲種電匠合格證照

Figure 89. Certificate of electrician of A grade.

圖 90　台電公司於工地佈線，提供臨時用電的態樣。

Figure 90. Scene of wiring of temporary power has been supplied by TPC to work site.

圖 91　工地臨時用電的變壓器需做隔離保護及警告標示防止感電意外發生

Figure 91. Tranformer should be isolated & protected with warning sign to prevent the electrical shock occure at work site.

圖 92　工地分電箱均採上鎖管理暨箱蓋張貼維修相關人員電話及明確標示

Figure 92. Distribution panel post the telephone of mainteinnance person & site office with definite warning signs on the cover.

圖 93　工地用改良型臨時分電箱外掛防水插座（110V//220V）的態樣

Figure 93. Improved type of distribution panel that mounted the plug sockets of water proof on each side board for using

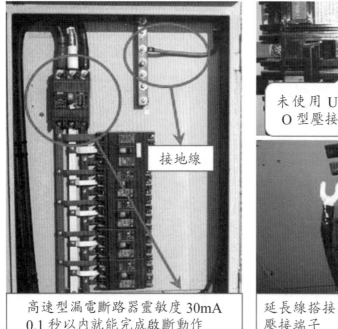

接地線

高速型漏電斷路器靈敏度 30mA
0.1 秒以內就能完成啟斷動作

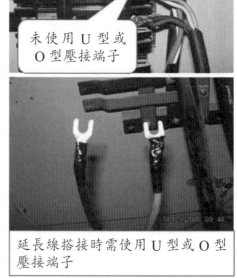

未使用 U 型或
O 型壓接端子

延長線搭接時需使用 U 型或 O 型
壓接端子

圖 94　依法規規定工地臨時分電箱內總開關及分路開關的標準器具配置

Figure 94. According the electric regulation that devices of master switch & shunt switch which meets the requirement in the temporary distribution panel

三相三線式用漏電斷路器

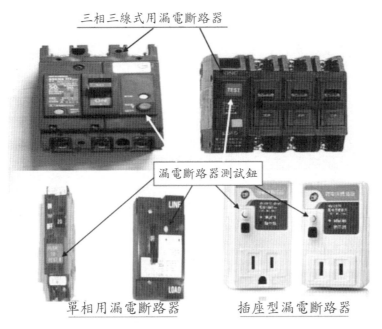

漏電斷路器測試鈕

單相用漏電斷路器　　　插座型漏電斷路器

圖 95　工地臨時分電箱內各分路開關的標準配置

Figure 95. Leakage Circuit Breaker of various types is essentialed to dispose of shunt switch in the temporary distribution panel.

標準設施（防風防水型）

圖 96　室外臨時分電箱外掛的插座需具有防水功能

Figure 96. Distribution panel at outside that mounted the plug sockets should have the function of water resistant.

電氣機具金屬製外殼連接綠色接地線

圖 97　工地臨時電氣機具均需外殼接地

Figure 97. Electrical facilities should mount the ground wire of exterior shell at work site.

圖 98　鋼筋作業切斷機的開關無護蓋防水，容易發生感電事故。

Figure 98. Re-bar cutter of reinforcement work which switch has no cover to prevent water that is easily to cause electric shock to workers.

圖 99　作業人員不得使用裸線叉接插座，容易造成感電意外發生。

Figure 99. Workers should not use the naked core wire to insert the socket that caused the electric shock accident easily.

圖 100　進場作業手工具均需通過漏電檢測器檢查合格才可使用

Figure 100. All handy tools of workers should be past by the leakage test machine for using.

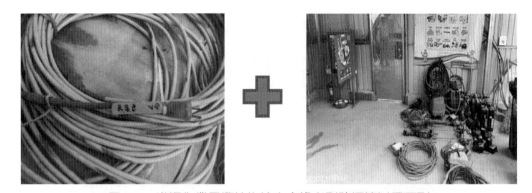

圖 101　進場作業電纜線均檢查合格者則貼標籤以示區別

Figure 101. Electric wire has tied the tag which as qualified in safety after testing.

圖 102　進場作業人員手工具必須經漏電檢測器檢查合格後貼標籤

Figure 102. Hand tool of worker must be test in qualified for tag by leakage test machine.

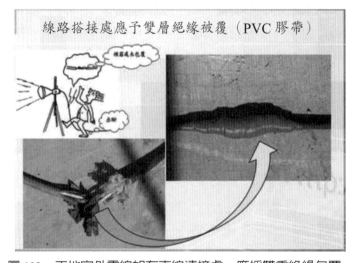

圖 103　工地室外電線如有直線連接處，應採雙重絕緣包覆。

Figure 103 Wires in outdoor that splice of wires connection should have dual wrapped.

圖 104　鄰近工區外的電線需用絕緣護套以防止感電發生

Figure 104. Power circuit line which was adjacent the work site should use insulating sheath to cover up for shock prevention.

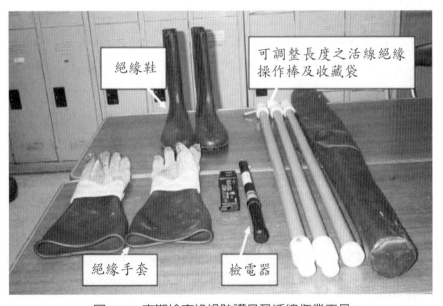

圖 105　定期檢查絕緣防護具及活線作業工具

Figure 105. Periodic Examine the isolation PPE & tools of live line.

圖 106　室內臨時電線均採高掛方式，不得置放於地面。

Figure 106. Power lines of indoor could not laid on the floor that are should hang under the ceiling for safety.

圖 107　室內臨時電線均採架牆吊掛方式，不得置放於地面。

Figure 107. Power lines of indoor should not lie on the ground that must be placed on the wall hanger for safety.

圖 108　室外臨時電線均採架高吊掛方式，不得置放於地面。

Figure 108. Power lines of outdoor could not lie on the ground that should hang on the hanger for safety.

圖 109　柴油發電機於作業前需點檢接地裝置

Figure 109. Grounding rods with device of diesel oil generators for welding should be check prior the work operation.

電纜線接續採用正確的壓接端子如 U/O 型

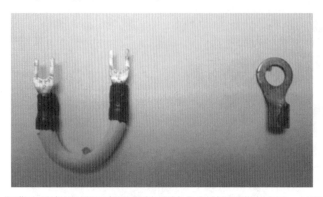

圖 110　作業區電焊機端子與電纜線銜接必須使用壓接端子 (U 型／O 型)

Figure 110. Crimping terminals as type of U/O should be used for electric cables of arc welding machine at job site.

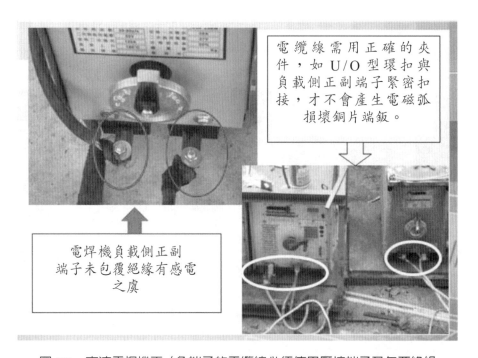

電纜線需用正確的夾件，如 U/O 型環扣與負載側正副端子緊密扣接，才不會產生電磁弧損壞銅片端鈑。

電焊機負載側正副端子未包覆絕緣有感電之虞

圖 111　交流電焊機正／負端子的電纜線必須使用壓接端子及包覆絕緣

Figure 111. Terminal of positive / negative connected the crimping terminals of power cables that terminals should be wraped to isolated with materials of AC arc welding machine.

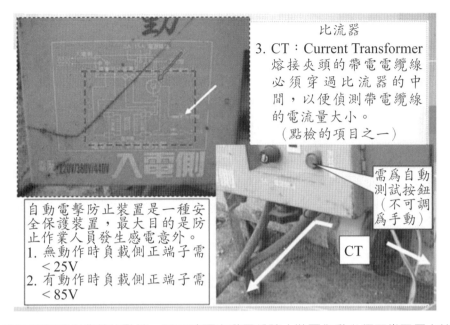

圖 112　交流電焊機作業前的點檢，是要確認自動電擊防止裝置作動必須正常及電力線必須穿過比流器。

Figure 112. Major checking point of prior operation that identify the function in normal of voltage reducing device for AC arc welding machine & power line should pass through the current transformer.

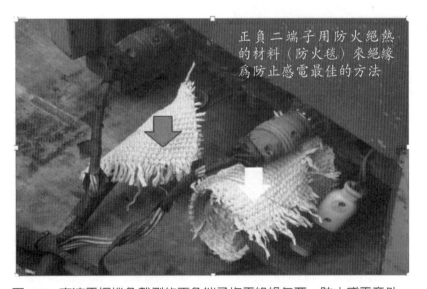

圖 113　交流電焊機負載側的正負端子均需絕緣包覆，防止感電意外。

Figure 113. Terminal of positive / negative of AC arc welding machine in output loading should be wrapped by isolate materials to prevent the shock accient.

電焊人員必須穿戴個人防護具防止感電意外

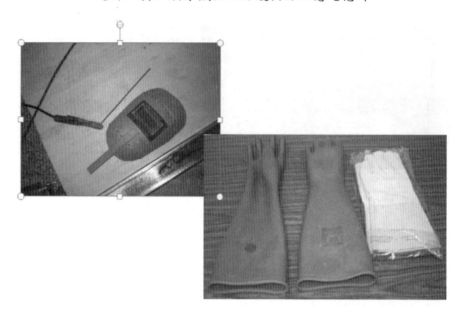

圖 114　電焊人員於電焊作業時，個人防護具必須穿戴完整。

Figure 114. Welder should put on the PPE (personal protective equipment) completely on the welding work.

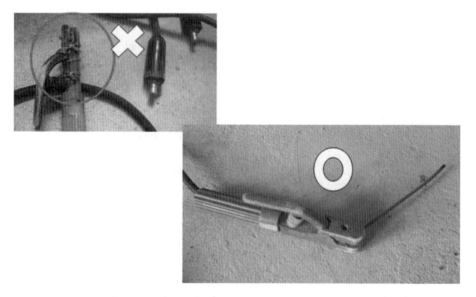

圖 115　電焊鉗的絕緣保護如破損必須更新，防止人員發生感電。

Figure 115. Protect cover of electrode holder which was broken that should be changed for new one to prevent the shock accident.

使用電焊機作業前，需檢點完成及個人防護具穿戴齊全。

圖 116　防止電焊作業發生感電，電焊人員於作業前針對電焊機具與個人防護具穿戴，應是必要的檢點作業。

Figure 116. To prevent the welder in shock accident that is to check the welding equipment & worn complete PPE & harness are essential work.

5-4 倒塌崩塌防制的關鍵要領 Crucial skill of prevention for collapse & tumble down

一、工地不同分項作業發生倒塌意外的圖片 Pictures of collapse incident in different works of sector at work site

圖 117　工地施工架全部倒塌影響公共安全

Figure 117. Scene of scaffold collapsed on the main artery that influenced the public safety.

圖 118　系統施工架倒塌，造成人員死亡職災。

Figure 118. Scene of systemic scaffold collapsed to cause the worker in death of occupational disaster.

圖 119　施工架因固定繫件鬆脫被破壞，經強風吹襲即將倒塌的態樣。

Figure 119. Scene of scaffolding with nets had been collapsed by strong wind in blowing due to the connectors were loosen & broken.

施工架發生挫曲照片

第二層施工架

第一層施工架

圖 120　施工架部分組合單元因材料堆放的集中荷重，造成立架發生挫曲。

Figure 120. Scaffold occurred the appearance of buckling due to the concentration loading where materials of mason which lay on the each layer at same position.

施工架材料側向位移導致破壞倒塌態樣

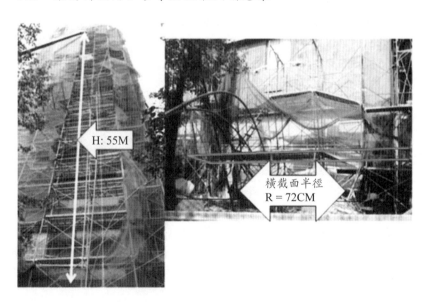

H: 55M

橫截面半徑
R = 72CM

圖 121　施工架因發生側向位移，造成壁連座固定件鬆脫有倒塌之虞。

Figure 121. Connectors were plucked up from the wall which was going to be collapsed that scaffold cased the displacement of lateral stress.

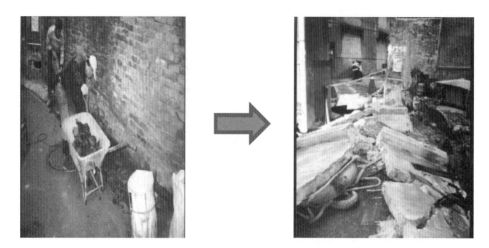

圖 122　工人清潔工區周邊的水溝而因磚牆倒塌致死的態樣

Figure 122. Worker cleaned the ditch where aside the work site that he was depressed under the break wall to died.

圖 123　工區模板材料堆垜的高度超過 180CM 容易造成倒塌意外事件

Figure 123. There was collapsed easily that wooden forms piled up which height more than 180cm at work site.

圖 124　工區柱牆單面模板組立，因斜撐不足遭強風吹倒造成虛驚事故。

Figure 124. Single wall forms were fallen down with gust to hurt the worker at site due to the angle bracing were not enough.

圖 125　地下室進行水平支撐的中間樁切除，因 H 型鋼倒塌造成工人死亡職災事故。

Figure 125. Worker was doing the cutting work to king pile as H shape steel at basement then steel fallen down to hit the worker to die.

圖 126　地下室地樑鋼筋紮結作業時突然倒塌造成職災死亡事故

Figure 126. Works of reinforcing bar erected for girder of basement that suddenly collapse to cause the fatal accident to steel workers.

圖 127　柱鋼筋紮結完成經強陣風吹襲倒塌的態樣

Figure 127. Column of rebar works were finished but it collapsed with strong gust.

二、施工架分項作業 Scaffold sectoral work

(一)施工架安全管理作業注意要點 Key point of safety management of scaffold

1. 落實施工架及上下設備的每日安全檢查，確保設施安全，將缺失減至最少。

2. 建立一個警告回報機制，有關施工架及上下設備被拆卸的缺失被察覺，均需立即回報地點及即時復歸缺失處，達到安全的要求。

3. 針對現場施工架的過度組裝，需定期授予安全課程及新的檢查方法，增高及部分區域的走道封閉，均需張貼警告標示。

4. 定期清理施工架、上下設備的混凝土殘泥及廢棄物，均需清理乾淨防止飛落意外發生。

5. 定期檢查是為達到設備的功能及使用的安全，因此設施如有缺陷不符合安全要求，應採汰舊換新的作業。

(二)施工架組立作業前應該注意要點 Key point of prior to erect the scaffold

1. 材料型式、規格及施工架構造型式均需檢查。

2. 載重條件及強度計算。

3. 地面承載條件。

4. 托架設置要求。

5. 與構造物連接。

6. 施工架加強措施。

7. 施工作業主管在現場調派及監督之責。

8. 壁連座及相關配件均需符合法規要求。

(三)施工架防制倒塌關鍵對策的圖片 Excellence images as crucial strategy of collapse incident prevention at work site

圖 128　施工架作業人員穿戴背負式安全帶

Figure 128. Workers erected the scaffold that should embrace the full body harness.

圖 129　施工架作業主管於現場督導作業人員組裝及檢查

Figure 129. Supervisor should have observation & inspection at site when the scaffold had been erected in progressing.

圖 130　施工架作業人員進行構件檢查及維修

Figure 130. Worker was check & maintain in progressing the scaffold at site.

圖 131　施工架組立範圍可規劃澆注混凝土作為鋪面

Figure 131. Planing the scope of scaffold erected where the bed course can place the concrete.

圖 132　施工架基底如是級配可用槽鋼做墊材，達到均布荷重的目的。

Figure 132. Base as aggregates beneath the scaffold erected where U shape steel be used under course to achieve the distributed loading.

圖 133　施工架的墊材可使用板材防止不均勻沉陷，避免倒塌意外。

Figure 133. Plank was used as bed course of scaffold which it can prevent the ununiform settlement occurred & collapse accident happen.

圖 134　依照法令規定，施工架必須外掛防塵網，但要考慮風壓的安全問題。

Figure 134. According the provisions that dust prevent nets should be spread & tight on the exterior of scaffold but safety issues must be concerned of blast pressure.

圖 135　颱風來臨時外掛防塵網必須綑捲，以防風壓造成施工架倒塌意外。

Figure 135. The dust prevent nets should be strapped of scaffold before the typhoon approaching otherwise collapse accident would be occurred with blast pressure.

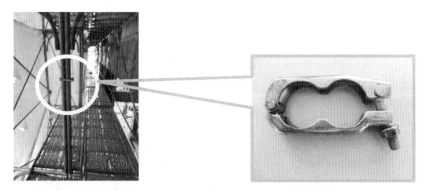

圖 136　施工架的立架相互併接時，應採用八字扣接合加勁。

Figure 136. Erecting frame of scaffold split to other erecting frame should used 8 shape of clamp for stiffness.

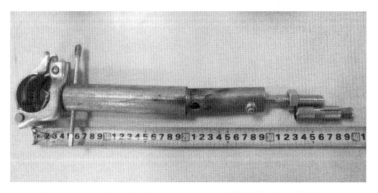

圖 137　壁連座是連接施工架與結構體的固定鐵件

Figure 137. Wall anchor with accessories was essential to link the structure concrete & clamp with the scaffold.

圖 138 防止施工架倒塌，壁連座的固定需維持水平狀態。

Figure 138. Preventing the collapse accident of scaffold that wall anchor & accessories should be fixing in same space of horizontal position.

圖 139 施工架壁連座的間距垂直線在 9M 以內及水平線在 8M 以內。

Figure 139. Wall anchor with scaffold which was fix spacing should be under the length as 9M in vertical line & 8M in horizontal line as required.

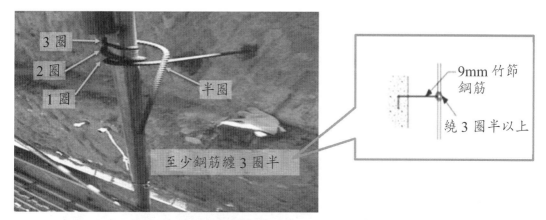

圖 140　施工架與結構體繫牆桿可採用 #3 鋼筋纏繞 3 圈半後，下摺固定。

Figure 140. Steel rods of D10 could be used as linkage between scaffold & structure that was to tied in 3 & half circles then bent down.

圖 141　施工架繫牆桿可採室內 GIP 立桿方式固定如圖示

Figure 141. Linkages as made as picture that was used the GIP with swivel clamps at indoor.

圖 142　防止施工架倒塌與鋼骨結構下翼鈑繫牆桿安全的作法

Figure 142. Preventing the collapse accident that linkage of GIP with accessories as C shape clip with swivel was clamped link the scaffold to the lower flange of H beam.

圖 143　施工架上下設備與鋼骨結構繫牆桿安全的作法如圖示

Figure 143. Access ladder of scaffold for steel structure which was linkage with swivel C shape clip to clamped to the beam in safety way of doing as picture.

圖 144　施工架為防止倒塌意外發生，可用斜撐加勁。

Figure 144. Used the GIP for bracing to the scaffold as stiff force added.

圖 145　施工架 GIP 管的斜撐加勁底部固定作法如圖示

Figure 145. The critical way of GIP was fix to bottom with swivel as stiff force as picture.

圖 146　遵照環保法令第 11 條工地抑制粉塵，施工架必須張掛防塵網。

Figure 146. Obligated the Environment Protection Regulation that scaffold should hang up the anti-dust nets completely to prevent dust spread in anywhere.

圖 147　颱風來襲前，考量施工架防塵網恐因風壓造成倒塌，逐應將防塵網綑紮起來。

Figure 147. Preventing the collapse which caused by blast pressure of scaffold so anti-dust nets should be wrapped in safety prior the typhoon approaching.

三、模板、鋼筋、混凝土分項作業 Sectoral works of form、rebar & concrete

模板、鋼筋、混凝土是三位一體，成為營建結構體最主要的材料，施工作業過程中，均需依照國家標準規範施工，但為什麼施工過程的前、中、後，仍然會發生倒塌意外，發生職災意外的遺憾。總結來說，包括材料不符合規定、施作程序未符合標準作業程序、天候因素、人為及外力等因素所造成的。遂各分項作業的前、中、後步驟均需要注意及落實。如否，則有可能發生工程災變。

圖 148　可調鋼管支撐失敗，發生工程倒塌的態樣。

Figure 148. Scene of construction's slab collapse due to the fail of tubular steel adjustable shore.

圖 149　地下室結構地樑的鋼筋紮結倒塌的態樣

Figure 149. Scene of girders of rebars work were collapsed in the basement structure.

(一) 模板、鋼筋、混凝土作業安全管理注意要點 Key point of safety management for the works of form、rebar & concrete

1. 倒塌災害防止對策：

   (1) 臨時構造強度分析。

   (2) 分項作業計畫風險評估。

   (3) 施工順序方法管理。

   (4) 施工作業方法改良。

   (5) 作業主管現場監督。

   (6) 落實優質作業管理。

   (7) 天候預知及掌握。

2. 災害防止對策：

   (1) 經濟原則：對策效應評估。

   (2) 有效原則：安全設施本質安全。

   (3) 可行原則：安全設施、經濟、有效綜合判定。

   (4) 選擇原則：安全設計、安全裝置、警告標誌。

   (5) 必行原則：安全衛生教育訓練（進場危害告知）。

(二)模板作業倒塌危害要因分析 Causal effect analysis of collapse hazard for forms work

表 6　模板作業主要部分危害要因分析

Chart6. Causal effect was analysised of hazard in major parts of formwork.

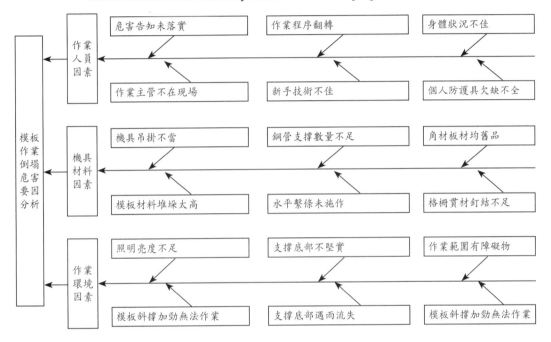

(三)模板作業防制倒塌關鍵對策的圖片 Excellence images as crucial strategy of form to prevent the collapse incident at work site.

圖 150　地下結構牆內側單面模板必須以可調式單鋼管斜撐固定

Figure 150. Single-sided wooden forms as interior of substructure have been strutted as angle by tubular steel adjustable shore.

圖 151　結構牆單面模板豎立完成必須以角材斜撐固定

Figure 151. Single-sided wooden form had been erected & bracing by timber.

圖 152　結構柱模板豎立完成必須以斜撐鐵桿固定

Figure 152. All-sided wooden form had been erected & bracing by steel rod.

圖 153　斜撐鐵桿的底部固結於模板上以加強勁度

Figure 153. Bracing rod which bottom plate has been fixed on the piece wooden form with nail to enforce the stiff strength.

圖 154　進場的可調鋼管支柱材料於使用前必須完成自動檢查

Figure 154. Materials of tubular steel adjustable shore should self-inspect the quality prior using to the form work.

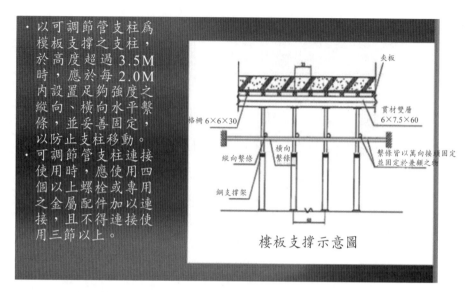

• 以可調節管支柱爲模板支撐之支柱，於高度超過 3.5M 時，應於每 2.0M 內設置足夠強度之縱向、橫向水平繫條，並妥善固定，以防止支柱移動。
• 可調節管支柱連接使用時，應使用四個以上螺栓或專用之金屬配件加以連接，且不得連接使用三節以上。

夾板

貫材雙層
6×7.5×60

格柵 6×6×30

縱向繫條　橫向繫條

鋼支撐架

繫條皆以萬向接頭固定
並固定於兼顧之物

樓板支撐示意圖

圖 155　依照法令支撐高度 > 350CM 必須於 200CM 下要有縱向及橫向水平繫條

Figure 155. Comply the ordinances which high of tubular steel adjustable shore (TSAS) over the 350CM to prevent (TSAS) displacement that there were bracing of horizentals & verticals direction less than 200CM in height.

圖 156　傳統樑版模板支柱作法潛存高風險墜落危害因子

Figure 156. Wooden forms with tubular steel adjustable shore (TSAS) of traditional working method that has high potential hazard of fall in the works.

圖 157　高風險樑模的組裝改採地上組裝方式，以降低墜落的風險。

Figure 157. To reduced the fall risk that form workers alter the procedure of assembled the wooden forms of beam on the ground.

圖 158　作業區樑模組裝完成依序排列在地上的態樣

Figure 158. Scene of wooden forms of beams which had been completed is on the ground.

圖 159　樑模組裝完成後，利用移動式起重機進行吊掛安放，並於兩端釘固的態樣。

Figure 159. The beam formwork has been finished on the ground that using the mobile crane to hoist the beam on fixed position & nailed firmly with workers in both end.

圖 160　樑模兩端與柱模釘固完成後，即用可調式鋼管支撐底模。

Figure 160. After wooden beams have been fixed to the both ends of column then workers used the tubular steel adjustable shore to the bottom of beams.

圖 161　樓板襯板底下的格柵及貫材需與可調式鋼管的上頂鈑相互釘固在一起

Figure 161. Rectangular & joist were nailed with top plates of tubular steel adjustable shore were nailed together in firm beneath liner plates.

圖 162　樓板塑膠襯板及樑模均完成釘結的態樣

Figure 162. Scene of plastic shuttering of slab with beams forms have been nailed firmly together.

圖 163　樓板鋼筋吊放至襯板上必須分開堆置，以防止集中荷重支撐挫曲發生。

Figure 163. To prevent the buckling of steel shore that slab rebar have been placed with hoisting gear on the slab where should put in separate location.

圖 164　樓板鋼筋堆置如產生集中荷重時，將造成鋼管支撐發生挫曲現象。

Figure 164. Some of steel shores caused the buckling appearance due to the Slab rebar stacked to much which loading over the bear capacities of steel shores.

圖 165　樓板高度超過 3.5M 時，鋼管支撐需設置縱向及橫向的水平繫條。

Figure 165. Comply the ordinances which height of tubular steel adjustible shore (TSAS) over 3.5M that fastened timbers should set up in the direction of verticle & horizontal.

圖 166 鋼管支撐超過 3.5M 高度時，支撐於 2M 處需設置縱向及橫向的水平繫條。

Figure 166. When the steel shores which height more than 3.5M then fastened timbers should set up in the direction of vertical & horizontal at 2M in high.

圖 167 縱向及橫向的水平繫條應與結構體切實連結，以防止鋼管支撐支柱移位。

Figure 167. End of fastened timbers for horizontal & verticle that there were connected the wall of structure to prevent the steel shore a bit shifting.

圖 168 鋼管支撐縱向及橫向的水平繫條端部與結構體切實連結的態樣

Figure 168. Scene of fastened timbers for horizontal & verticle which end connected certainly the structure.

(四) 業界推出的新系統模板工法 There was new systemic formwork which was provided & utilitied to some contractors of construction field.

由於營建業近年來從事現場模板作業人員年齡增長及體弱力衰等諸多因素,造成工地模板工逐漸凋零,進而影響整體工程進度。遂有企圖心的業者也開始研發使用不同的材料,以標準化、規格化的單元為基本構件,系統化的組裝作業,達到效率化的進度目標。最主要的成果是材料可以循環再利用,達到政府推動節能、減碳、環保的政策。

2010 節能減碳年標誌　　節能標章　　省水標章

環保標章　　碳足跡標章　　綠建材標章

圖 169　結構柱採鋁製系統模板組立完成的態樣

Figure 169.Scene of column were completed with systemic forms works of aluminum

圖 170　為防止倒塌柱鋁模板組立完成後，均用鐵桿斜撐。

Figure 170. To prevents the collapse of column which used the steel rod to brace.

圖 171　結構柱牆及樑採鋁製系統模板組立完成並採斜撐的態樣

Figure 171. Sence of column wall & beam which were assembled completely with aluminum forms work & steel rod to brace.

圖 172　結構柱牆採鋁製系統模板組立作業及施工架作業平台等設施

Figure 172. Structure of column & wall has been installed with aluminum formworks system & platform of scaffold installations.

圖 173　塑膠製系統模板堆放於工區以利結構體牆模使用的態樣

Figure 173. Scene of material of formwork has been stacked at site for the wall installation of structure as concrete operations.

圖 174　柱牆使用塑膠製系統模板完成的態樣

Figure 174. Scene of column & wall has been completed with plastics made of formwork system.

圖 175　第一階層系統模板組裝使用特別的斜撐支架之態樣

Figure 175. Formworks system was assembled in the 1st grade on the concrete floor with special facilities of push-pull props for safety.

圖 176　廠房第一階層系統模板已完成混凝土澆注後，進行第二階層系統模板組立態樣。

Figure 176. After concrete have pour completely in 1st grade elevated of formworks system, then 2nd grade elevated formworks system was in progressing.

(五)鋼管施工架（框式施工架）為模板支撐支柱作業前應注意要點 Key points as prior work of scaffolding erect as many layers (framed bent) that are to shoring up the formworks.

1. 支撐構件材料型式、規格及構造型式
2. 載重條件及強度計算
3. 地面承載條件
4. 組立順序及臨時固定
5. 調整底座、托架、貫材安置及調整注意事項
6. 斜撐及橫撐等加強措施
7. 與模板銜接處施工注意事項

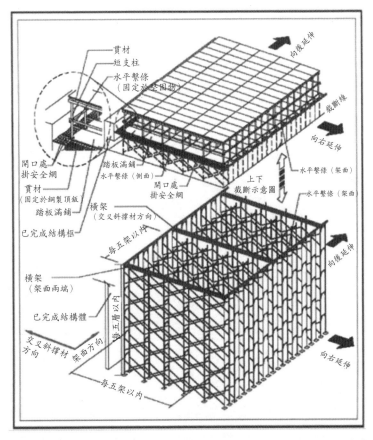

圖 177　營造安全衛生設施標準第 136 條圖示鋼管施工架（框式施工架）的規定

Figure 177. Comply the ordinances of article 136 of construction safety health facilities standards that describe the related regulation of framed bent.

圖 178　鋼管施工架（框式施工架）接合鋼管支撐支柱必須施作縱向及橫向的水平繫條防止
　　　　移位

Figure 178. There was fastened timbers for horizontal & verticle to prevent the shifting with steel shore which on the framed bent.

圖 179　鋼管施工架（框式施工架）組立時為防止作業人員墜落，應張掛安全網。

Figure 179. When scaffolds were erected & joined together to more layers that should spread the safety nets on the proper height to prevent the fall accident.

圖 180　鋼管施工架（框式施工架）組立時要設置上下樓梯，以利組裝作業。

Figure 180. Stairway should erect to workers when they erected & joined the scaffolds in progressing.

圖 181　框式施工架在組立時，要預留人員安全通道及明顯箭頭標示。

Figure 181. During the work of framed bent that safety path for workers should reserve with obvirous direction arrow.

圖 182 縱向及橫向水平繫條的端部均需抵觸牆或柱面，以防止水平位移。

Figure 182. Fastened steel pipes of horizontal & verticle on the scaffolds that prevent the horizontal shift which end plate should be connect firmly to the structure.

圖 183 鋼管施工架（框式施工架）依規定設置縱向及橫向水平繫條的態樣

Figure 183. Scene of fastened steel pipes of horizontal & vertical were to interlock on the scaffolds.

圖 184　鋼管施工架（CNS4750）為模板支撐，支撐底部應設置可調型基腳座鈑。

Figure 184. Scaffolds are fit the regulation of CNS4750 which erect & join as framed bent for the formwork shoring that is initial to install the adjustable base plate to rod.

(六) 鋼筋作業倒塌危害要因分析 Causal effect analysis of collapse hazard for rebar works

1. 鋼筋混凝土結構中，鋼筋有如人體骨骼的角色，鋼筋加工組立之目的，係在使鋼筋經由切割、彎曲、接續、運搬、吊放、綁紮、固定等步驟，將鋼筋製成設計的形狀及紮結在柱、牆、板正確的位置，以達成結構構架，各個構件預期的結構行為。工地鋼筋組立作業經常在高處作業，或在深開挖處作業，與模板工程、水電配管工程及其他預埋件等作業有密切相互依賴性與重疊性。

2. 鋼筋組立作業潛在危害，其災害類型有：(1) 感電；(2) 飛落；(3) 倒塌；(4) 割擦傷，其災害防止對策必需於作業前將潛在危害因子予以排除，才能達到零災害的目的。

   (1) 感電的防止對策：

   　A. 電氣設備應裝設合於設備需求之漏電斷器。

   　B. 用電設備及電線應定期檢查壓扣開關必須具有防水功效。

   　C. 吊車作業人員應對作業環境進行危害辨識並採行控制措施。

   　D. 對於吊車作業範圍內之電線應施予標示及設置護圍、裝設絕緣掩蔽或遷移線路等措施。

   (2) 飛落的防止對策：

A. 加強安全衛生教育訓練。

B. 僱用合格之起重機操作人員。

C. 人員之精神狀態應予注意。

D. 鋼材吊升時要用拉索穩定防止擺盪，其他人員撤離起重機作業半徑。

(3) 倒塌的防止對策：

A. 鋼筋之接續、連接，無論為電銲、壓接，或以聯結器聯結均應確實。

B. 鋼筋結構在組合過程中均應視其穩定情況以斜撐、拉索或其他有效方法加以支撐。

(4) 割擦傷的防止對策：

A. 作業時配戴手套。

B. 搬運時儘量使用輔助工具或起重機具。

C. 不得已須抬舉、人工搬運時，以安全姿勢為之。

表 7　鋼筋作業主要部分危害要因分析表

Chart7. Causal effect analysis of hazard in major parts for rebar works.

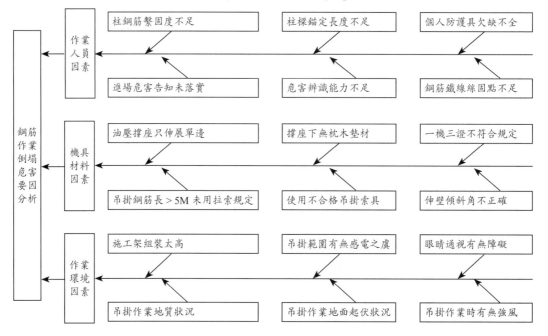

圖 185　鋼筋裁剪機的開關必須有防水盒才能防止感電意外

Figure 185. The power switch which cover should has waterproof to prevent the shock accident of rebar shear cutting.

圖 186　螺旋筋箍筋成型機於作業前檢點接地是必要項目

Figure 186. Grounding of machine as shaped spiral stirrup which was initial items of checking prior operation.

圖 187　鋼筋作業的繫筋禁止用鋼筋彎折支架裝載吊運

Figure 187. Prohibited tie bars were bank up on the hanger of rebar bent to lifting to the rebar work at work site.

圖 188　鋼筋作業的繫筋或箍筋應用吊籃裝載吊運

Figure 188. Tie bars & stirrups should are bank up in the hanging bracket for hoisting to worksites.

圖 189　進行地下結構鋼筋作業時，鋼筋不得暫置支撐鋼樑上方，容易造成倒塌意外事件。

Figure 189. Rebars of typical length should not lay on the horizontal struct to prevent the collapse accident happen of rebar woks of substructure.

圖 190　地下結構的柱預留筋均需塑膠帽套，以防穿刺意外發生。

Figure 190. Retained rebar which end parts of column should has plastic cap in each rebar to prevent the puncture accident at substructure.

圖 191　鋼筋作業人員必須戴手套，防止手指發生夾傷意外。

Figure 191. Workers should were the gloves to prevent the injury of fingers as pinch.

圖 192　為防止柱鋼筋因受風力影響彎曲倒塌，作業人員使用施工架進行箍筋圍束作業。

Figure 192. To prevent the rebar to bent & collapsed with blowing wind that rebar workers were to tie the stirrups to the rebar of column with scaffold.

圖 193　地下結構柱牆鋼筋作業完成的態樣

Figure 193. Scene of rebar works of column with wall in the substructure.

圖 194　柱鋼筋紮結作業需設置安全的施工架作業平台之態樣

Figure 194. Scene of installed the safety platforms of scaffold to the rebar works as column erected.

圖 195　鋼筋工依照鋼筋撿料單進行樓板樑鋼筋組立紮結作業

Figure 195. Steel fixers according to the rebar picking slip to assembled rebars with the tired wire for beams of slab.

圖 196　工地樓板的柱、樑、版鋼筋組立紮結完成的態樣

Figure 196. The scene of rebar work to column、beam & slab which have been completed at site.

(七) 混凝土作業倒塌危害要因分析 Causal effect analysis of collapse hazard for concrete work

1. 法令依據：

(1) 職業安全衛生設施規則第 120 條：對於車輛系營建機械，如作業時有因該機械翻落、

表土崩塌等危害勞工之虞者，應於事先調查該作業場所之地質、地形狀況等，適當決定下列事項或採必要措施，並將第一款至第四款事項告知作業勞工：一、所使用車輛系營建機械之種類及性能。二、車輛系營建機械之行經路線。三、車輛系營建機械之作業方法。四、整理工作場所以預防該等機械之翻倒、翻落。

(2) 職業安全衛生設施規則第 121 條：雇主對於車輛系營建機械之修理或附屬裝置之安裝、拆卸等作業時，應就該作業指定專人負責下列措施：一、決定作業順序並指揮作業。二、監視於機臂，突樑下作業之勞工所使用安全支柱、絞車等之狀況。

2. 壓力輸送車之輸送管依其配設方式可區分為：

(1) 配管式──以鋼管及管夾組裝成輸送管，並固定於營建物建構體或施工架之外側，在模板上方之輸送管則墊以廢輪胎，防止管之移位，末端連接軟管以方便移動澆置位置。由於模板上鋪設之輸送管會產生水平振動力而廢輪胎無法吸收該振動力，如模板結構不足以抵抗該水平力時，則易發生倒塌，此為配管式之最大缺點。

圖 197　工地將混凝土輸送管配設採取（直立式及水平式）配管式作法

Figure 197. Concrete delivery steel pipes have been installed as vertical & horizontal shapes for concrete pouring work at site.

(2) 桁架式──混凝土輸送車上裝設可伸縮（曲折）式之鋼製桁架，用以支撐並固定輸送管，作業時將桁架及其內側之輸送管延伸至預定澆置混凝土位置，而不需另設其支撐為其特徵。由於桁架式不與模板結構接觸，因此不會將輸送管之振動力傳送至模板支撐，此為其優點。但如果作業場所附近有高壓電線而桁架需接近該電路作業時，則有碰觸造成感電之虞，於此情況應防止感電以策安全。

圖 198　桁架式混凝土壓送車於作業前需檢點伸縮桁架是否正常

Figure 198. Truck mounted concrete boom pump that was to execute the self-inspection to boom with steel pipes which in normal condition prior the pouring concrete at site.

3. 潛在危害、災害類型、災害防止對策：

(1) 撞擊：車輛後退時壓輾施工、非施工人員或指揮人員，使人員撞擊受傷者或死亡。

防止對策：施工人員、指揮人員、配合工作者加強教育訓練，正確指揮位置、信號及隧道內任何人員一律穿反光衣，禁止非施工人員進入工作區。

(2) 車輛翻覆：在地基不穩處或斷壁附近作業。

防止對策：車輛在後退時作業，應有人員指揮以防掉落，準備混凝土澆置作業或收工時，應注意停放處地基是否穩固、牢靠、有無掉落之虞。

(3) 切割傷：作業時攪拌器護蓋開啟，人員滑落致為攪刀所傷。

防止對策：作業時攪刀護蓋不得開啟。

(4) 相關作業環境之危害：

A. 感電：桁架式壓力輸送車之輸送料臂及管線在架設及伸縮時觸高壓電，而發生感電事故。

防止對策：工作範圍之高壓電線予以遷移、設護圍或加絕緣保護，壓力輸送車接地。壓力輸送車輸送料臂及管線在架設及伸縮時，須派人指揮以免碰及電纜線而感電。

B. 倒塌：壓送車之輸送等垂直部分，如繫固於施工架，則因施工架各構件及其連結缺陷，在其壓送之振動力的作用力下造成鬆脫等，進而導致倒塌災害。另輸送管

水平管安置於模板上，則壓送時其水平振動力作用於模板支撐，如因支撐構件及其連結固定等缺陷而發生倒塌災害。

防止對策：(a) 避免利用施工架作為壓力輸送管之繫固、錨定，如不得已應加強施工架之各構件之平穩。(b) 妥為設計模板支撐結構系統，使其具抵抗壓力輸送管振動力之能力，或使用隔震裝置，使輸送管振動力不致傳送至模板支撐結構。

表 8　混凝土澆置作業主要部分危害要因分析表

Chart8. Causal effect analysis of hazard in major parts forconcrete pouring works

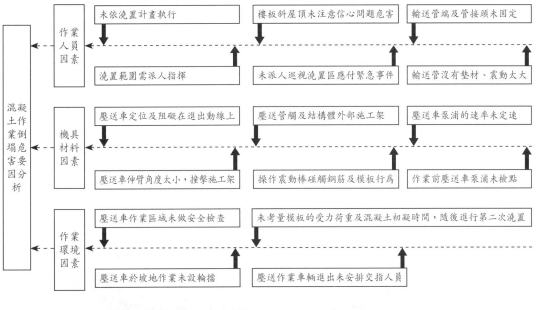

圖 199　派遣交通指揮手於馬路旁管控預拌混凝土車的安全

Figure 199. Traffic conductor who controlled the mixer truk stopped aside the road for pumping work.

圖 200　混凝土壓送車定位後先檢點壓送裝置及其他器具

Figure 200. Self-inspection was exected to the appliances after concrete pump truck fixed position.

圖 201　混凝土壓送車的油壓撐座必須完全伸出，以防意外發生。

Figure 201. Major rigger has been extended completely to prevent the incident occure prior the pouring concrete in progress.

圖 202　混凝土壓送車於斜坡上進行混凝土壓送的態樣

Figure 202. Scene of the concrete pump truck was operating the concrete pouring at ramp of road.

圖 203　混凝土壓送車於斜坡上作業時，必須把油壓撐座固定於地面。

Figure 203. Concrete pump truck should extend the rigger on the ground firmly when operated the concrete work at ramp of road.

圖 204　混凝土預拌車於斜坡上作業，必須放置輪擋防止滑動。

Figure 204. Placing the chock wheel to prevents the wheel rolling at ramp of road during the pouring work.

圖 205　混凝土壓送車攪拌器下方應張鋪帆布防止地面汙染

Figure 205. Spread the sheet of canvas under the agitator to keep the tidy of ground.

圖 206　混凝土壓送管裝置應用墊木固定防止鬆動

Figure 206. Appliances of steel delivery pipe which placed the sleeper in firm to prevent loose situation appearance.

圖 207　配合混凝土澆置作業錨定結構體的壓送管必須穩固

Figure 207. Steel delivery pipes were anchored firmly on the wall that matched the concrete pump truck.

圖 208 混凝土壓送車及預拌車如占用馬路作業需有交通錐警示

Figure 208. Placing the traffic cones for warning aside the pouring operation scoop where near by the road.

圖 209 混凝土預拌車的主要動線與材料堆置需有明顯區隔（如：交通錐警示）

Figure 209. There is obveriously separated with traffic cones on the route at site for mixer truck access & material deposited zone.

圖 210　混凝土澆置作業時，作業人員需相互使用對講機達到通聯效果。

Figure 210. During the concrete pouring works that workers shall use the intercom to contact to each others.

圖 211　混凝土進行樑澆置使用震動棒時，應注意作業平台的間隙防止墜落。

Figure 211. Workers are operating the vibrator during the pouring work that they shall pay attention of the gap on the scaffold.

圖 212　作業人員於施工架使用模外震動器時，應注意間隙防止意外發生。

Figure 212. Worker uses the form vibrator at scaffold that they shall pay attention of the gap of scaffold.

圖 213　混凝土進行樓板澆置時，應注意管夾是否固定安全。

Figure 213. When the pouring works on the slab that worker should check the pipe clamp which tightly
to the join portion of delivery pipes.

圖 214　混凝土進行澆置時，應注意混凝土噴漿的危害。

Figure 214. There was blast mortar as potential hazard during the concrete pouring work on the slab.

圖 215　混凝土壓送車的桁架壓送管下方禁止作業人員站立

Figure 215. Prohibited worker who stood the below of truck mounted concrete boom pump.

圖 216　桁架式混凝土壓送車進行樓板混凝土澆置的態樣

Figure 216. Scene of concrete slab was in pouring work with truck mounted concrete boom pump.

圖 217　現場使用軌道式電動整平機進行混凝土平整作業

Figure 217. Pouring concrete has been screeded to flate with power screed machine along the guide rails.

圖 218　軌道式電動整平器完成作業後，使用座騎式鏝光機粗磨壓實作業。

Figure 218. Worker held the riding style of concrete power trowel to compact & rough the concrete surface.

圖 219　作業人員使用手持式鏝光機進行細磨鏝光作業

Figure 219. Worker held the manual style of concrete power trowel to do as finest trowel work at site.

圖 220　現場使用不同的鏝光機進行整體粉光作業

Figure 220. There was two different styles of concrete power trowels in progress the work at site.

圖 221　泥作工於現場進行修補鏝光作業

Figure 221. Mason gripped the trowel to patch the surface of concrete in smooth.

圖 222　地坪經過整體粉光作業完成後的態樣

Figure 222. Science of entirety floor where has been troweled to smooth.

5-5 火災防制的關鍵要領 Crucial skill of prevention for fire accident

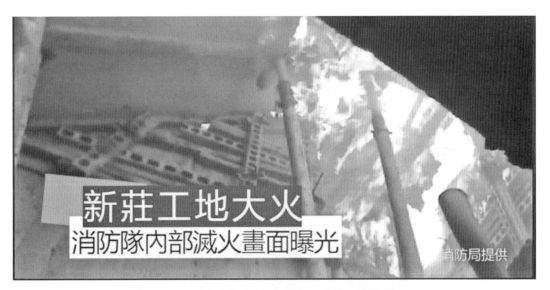

圖 223　工地火災的危害影響及損失更勝於戰場

Figure 223. The influence of hazard & damage of fire occurred at work site were seriously than the battle field.

一、火災的起因 Cause of fire as disaster.

工地火災發生的原因不外乎是人為動火作業的疏失、人為蓄意縱火、或自然災害如閃電雷擊所導致，然火災發生初期，因現場未準備及擺放滅火器或數量不足，以致失去初期控制火勢機會，而釀成重大火災，造成重大人員傷亡及財產損失。

火災為一種燃燒作用，亦為一種氧化反應，即將燃料與氧氣（含氧化劑）混合後，以火花或溫度引燃，並產生自由基而引發連鎖反應之化學作用，此種反應非常快速，除將產生燃燒產物外，另亦伴隨釋出熱能及火光。

二、火災種類 Types of fire as disaster..

火災依燃燒的物質之不同可分為四大類，分別說明如下：

(一) 普通火災 General type of fire as disaster

普通火災指木材、紙張、纖維、棉毛、塑膠、橡膠等之可燃性固體引起之火災。此類火災可以藉由水的冷卻作用降低燃燒溫度，以達滅火效果。

(二) 油類火災 Fuel / oil type of fire as disaster.

油類火災指石油類、有機溶劑、油漆類、油脂類等可燃性液體及可燃性固體引起之火災。最有效的是掩蓋法隔離氧氣，使之「窒熄」。此外，如移開可燃物或降低溫度，亦可達到滅火效果。

(三) 電氣火災 Electrical type of fire as disaster..

電氣火災指電氣配線、馬達、引擎、變壓器配電盤等通電中之電氣機械器具及電氣設備引起之火災。有時可用不導電的滅火劑控制火勢，但如能截斷電源再視情況依普通火災或油類火災處理，較為妥當。

(四) 特殊火災 Special fire as disaster..

特殊火災指鈉、鉀、鎂、鋰與鋯等可燃性金屬物質及禁水性物質引起之火災。這些物質燃燒時溫度甚高，須使用特殊金屬化學乾粉滅火劑撲滅。

三、火災燃燒及閃燃的要因 Causes of fire as burning & flashover.

當燃料、氧氣及溫度（即俗稱**燃燒三要素**）同時存在，燃燒才會發生。如固體類物質之燜燒模式，氧氣僅存於燜燒燃料表面，其所產生之熱量約有 2/3 將散至大氣環境中而消失。惟經過一段時期後，將因燃料與氧氣經由擴散以及燃燒產物自由基之快速增加，而使燃燒反應加速進行，且能自動連續再點燃而產生**連鎖反應**。

圖 224　燃燒三要素是燃料、氧氣及溫度

Figure 224. Flame which essential factors are fuel、oxygen、heat.

■ 三角錐理論
　◆ 燃料（可燃物）
　◆ 氧氣（助燃物）
　◆ 熱能（火源）
　◆ 連鎖反應

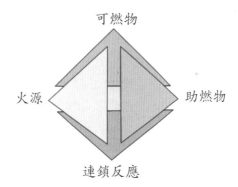

圖 225　燃燒三角錐理論

Figure 225.Triangular pyramid theory of combustio.

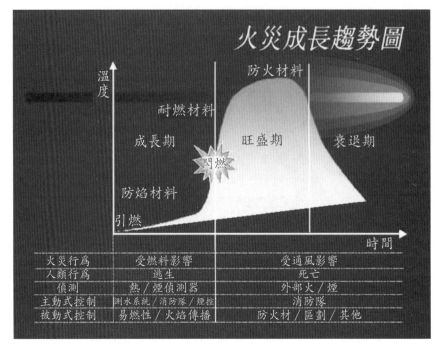

圖 226　火災成長趨勢圖

Figure 226. The trend chart of growing up on fire..

圖 227　閃燃原理的說明

Figure 227. Specification to the theory of flashover.

四、工地動火作業類別的說明 Illustration of categories that hot work at work site.

圖 228　砂輪機進行鐵管切割作業的態樣

Figure 228. The grinding wheel cut the pipe at site.

圖 229　氧氣乙炔切割器進行作業的態樣

Figure 229.Oxyacetylene cutter was cutting the steel beam at site.

圖 230　電焊工進行柱樑焊道熔接作業的態樣

Figure 230.Welder used arc welding machine to weld the joint of column & beam.

圖 231　電焊工利用電焊將筏基板鋼筋補強的作業態樣

Figure 231.Welder used the arc welding machine to the work as rebar reinforce at raft slab.

圖 232　水管工作業使用的強力噴燈

Figure 232. High power torch was used by plumber to the work.

圖 233　技術工使用電焊機進行消防管連接作業

Figure 233. Technician used the arc weld machine to welding the connection of fire steel pipe.

五、工地動火作業造成火災的潛因 There were potential factors that had hot works to cause the fire as a disaster at site.

圖 234 電焊作業的熔渣火花隨處掉落地面

Figure 234. The slag sparks were flutter down on the ground during the welding in progress.

圖 235 電焊作業的熔渣火花必須用防火毯承接

Figure 235. Slag sparks of welding work shoul be socked with fire blanket.

圖 236　模板材料進行動火作業容易造成火災

Figure 236. There was easily to cause fire on the woodern forms that was fire work on it.

圖 237　柴油發電機需定期保養才能防止機件著火

Figure 237. A diesel-electric set should have maintenance in term to prevent the components which on fire.

圖 238　電焊火花碰到達到飽和揮發性溶劑的泥土瞬間起火

Figure 238. Sparks of welding work were to flow on the soil where contain saturated volatile solvent that caused the soil on fire instantly.

六、工地防制火災發生的管理作法 Manners of management prevent the fire as disaster occurred at work sites.

(一) 工區進行動火作業的相關規定 Rated regulations of hot work in progressing at work site.

＊作業前向安衛單位申請
1. 作業時要有監火人員監視。
2. 滅火器要準備，且放置於明顯位置以便取用。
3. 任何摻有溶劑如甲苯、松香水、香蕉水等油料禁止亂倒。
4. 工具箱交談將加強宣導動火作業安全。

圖 239　監火人員必須於動火作業的現場執行監視責任

Figure 239. Observer of hot work should excuited the responsibility of observation at site.

切割機安全防護暨防火要項

圖 240　操作人員的個人防護具及機器的防護罩均需符合安全規定

Figure 240. Operator's personal protective equipment (PPE)& shield of grinding wheel which are to comply the safety regulation.

圖 241　氧氣及乙炔鋼瓶貯存區需分開安全置放及張貼安全資料表

Figure 241. Steel cylinder of oxygen & acetylene were placed to separate under the shed with obvious notice as Safety Data Sheet(SDS).

圖 242　氧氣乙炔切割操作在作業前需檢點相關配件是否功能正常如上圖

Figure 242. Identified the crucial accessories which the function normally prior the operation of oxy-
acetylene to fire cutting work.as above pictures.

注意事項

1. 先檢查作業區域內有無易燃物應移除或防護。
2. 設置防火措施（防火毯等）及設置監火人員，並於動火區域架設警戒圍籬。
3. 備妥滅火措施並確定有效。
4. 施工作業人員及監火人員是否具有動火防火之安全意識教育訓練。
5. 作業人員是否有配戴安全防護具（手套、護目鏡等）。
6. 施工作業前，有無完成作業之申請（動火作業申請單）。

圖 243　乾粉滅火器需定期每月檢查一次，確保壓力維持正常。

Figure 243. Powder extinguisher should has inspection in per month to assure the pressure in normal
condition.

七、工地滅火設備須知 Notice of fire extinguishtion equipments at work site.

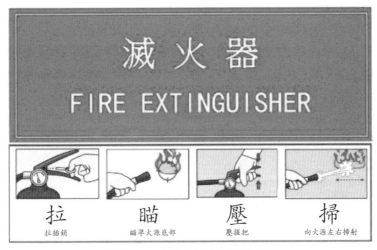

圖 244　乾粉滅火器使用口訣

Figure 244. A pithy formula of dry powered fire extinguisher to using.

內政部消防署已將使用 20 餘年的滅火器使用口訣更改為「拉、瞄、壓、掃」。

(一) 拉（插銷）：提起滅火器後，將安全插銷「旋轉並拉開」。

(二) 瞄（火源）：握住皮管噴嘴後，瞄準火源底部。

(三) 壓（握把）：用力握下手壓柄（壓到底），朝向火源根部噴射。

(四) 掃（向火源左右噴灑）：左右移動掃射後，持續監控並確定火源熄滅。

八、其他注意事項 Other items of attention.

(一) 火災發生時，應保持冷靜鎮定並使用工區內的乾粉滅火器進行滅火，如火勢無法控制時，立即通知周圍人員撤離，並且撥打 119 報案。報案時，應告知火災正確地址、人員所在樓層位置，以及有無人員受困。

(二) 一般火災可用水減災；如為油類及化學物品引起，不可用水，應用乾粉、二氧化碳等滅火器滅火。

(三) 使用滅火器時，應站在上風處，先拔插銷，噴嘴直接朝向火源底部噴灑藥劑，但萬一火勢擴大無法撲滅時，應立即進行避難。

(四) 進入樓層作業場所應先留意避難路線標示，確保兩方向避難出口位置。

(五) 為預防火災，於作業區範圍設置休息吸菸區，並擺放菸蒂筒及乾粉滅火器一罐，以備突發狀況發生時使用；電線插座不可插上太多插頭，插座要經常清除灰塵。

5-6 缺氧作業的關鍵要領 Crucial skill of work for hyposia operation

一、何謂缺氧 What is called of hypoxia.

一般正常空氣中氧氣濃度約 21%，如果在 18% 以下，作業有可能產生身體不舒適，在 16% 以下會造成人腦判斷力降低而易產生不安全行為，所以將氧氣濃度低於 18% 以下稱為缺氧危險作業。

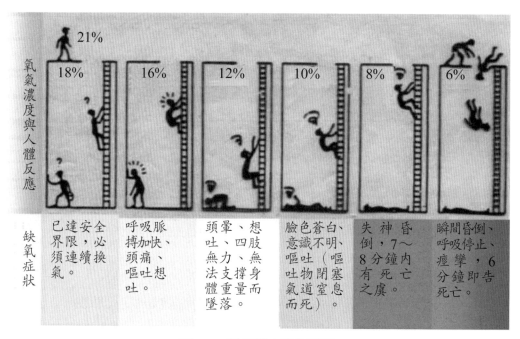

圖 245　缺氧對人體的反應

Figure 245. Reaction of human body to hypoxia.

二、何謂侷限空間 What is called of confined spaces.

指法律規定非供勞工在其內部從事經常性作業，勞工進出方法受限制，且無法以自然通風來維持充分、清淨空氣之空間。

圖 246　侷限空間入坑作業團隊合作訓練海報
Figure 246. Poster as training of teamwork that workers enter the pit to work at site.

(一) 侷限空間從事作業危害防止要點 Crucial point of prevent the hazard that has the work in the confine spance.

　　雇主使勞工於侷限空間從事作業前，應先確認該空間內有無可能引起勞工缺氧、中毒、感電、塌陷、被夾、被捲及火災、爆炸等危害，有危害之虞者，應訂定危害防止計畫，並使現場作業主管、監視人員、作業勞工及相關承攬人依循辦理。

　　缺氧危險作業危害防止計畫，應依作業可能引起之危害訂定下列事項：

1. 侷限空間內危害之確認。
2. 侷限空間內氧氣、危險物、有害物濃度之測定。
3. 通風換氣實施方式。
4. 電能、高溫、低溫及危害物質之隔離措施及缺氧、中毒、感電、塌陷、被夾、被捲等危害防止措施。
5. 作業方法及安全管制作法。
6. 進入作業許可程序。
7. 提供之防護設備之檢點及維護方法。
8. 作業控制設施及作業安全檢點方法。
9. 緊急應變處置措施。

(二) 侷限空間安全作業標準 Standard of safety operation in confined spaces

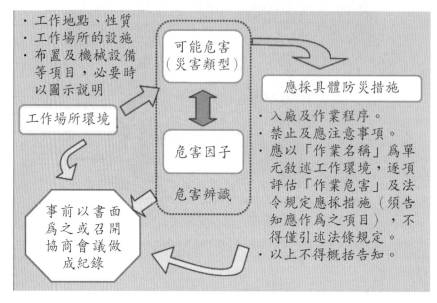

圖 247　侷限空間作業危害辨識分析圖

Figure 247. An analysis diagram of hazards identify which work is in the confined space.

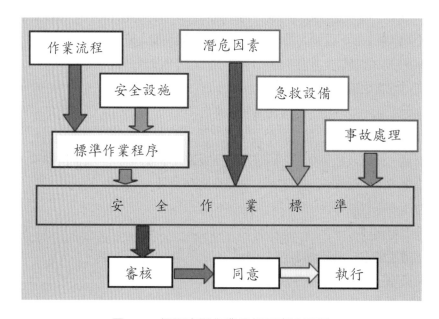

圖 248　侷限空間作業分析及審核流程

Figure 248. Work operation analysis & review flow of confined space.

(三) 工地筏基水池坑開口安全設施說明 Description of safety protectoral　facilities which to hatch of the pit as raft foundation at work site.

圖 249　筏基水池坑開口設置安全護欄

Figure 249. Guard rail had been installedaround the hatch of pit on the raft foundation.

圖 250　筏基坑開口以模板覆蓋及張貼警告標示

Figure 250. Hatch of pit was covered with wooden form copletely with warning notice.

(四)工地筏基水池坑（侷限空間）作業演練說明 Operation exercise of work in the pit of confined space at work site.

圖 251　作業前檢點相關設施（如三腳架配捲揚防墜器、通風換氣設施、個人防護具、送電開關含漏電斷路器、長鋁梯）及其他等

Figure 251. Self-inspection prior the work of confined space to workers that facilities have been check as (tripod fitted with self-retracting lifeline,airline assemblies & air pump,personal pertective equipment,no fuse power switch with leakage circuit breaker,aluminum step ladder) & others.

圖 252　通風設施擺放正確位置及送風測試

Figure 252. Flexible duct have been set at right place & switc on for ventilation.

圖 253　筏基坑通風換氣前後的氣體濃度數值進行比對

Figure 253. Figures of gas concentration with detector has been compaired as before & after of ventilator supply.

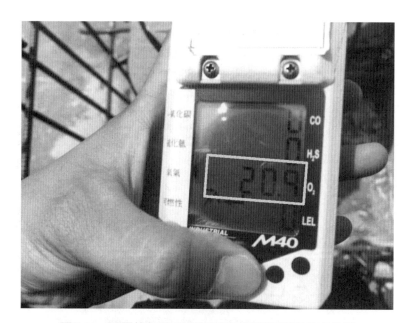

圖 254　通風換氣後的氧氣濃度偵測數值符合安全值

Figure 254. Detector data of oxygen concentration was to comply with a standard after the ventilator in operation.

圖 255　作業主管向入坑作業人員說明侷限空間安全作業要點

Figure 255. Chief of operation who spoke the safety point as confined space to workers who will do the work in the pit at work site.

圖 256　作業主管為入坑人員詳細檢查背負式安全帶

Figure 256. Chief of operation check the worker's full body harness before worker enter the pit to work.

圖 257　入坑人員於作業許可程序單上簽名認可的態樣

Figure 257. Worker signed the list of work permission & recognition to work in the pit.

圖 258　入坑人員經由吊升三腳架緩緩入坑作業

Figure 258. Worker enters slowly into the pit by tripod with hoist apparatus.

圖 259　入坑人員經由作業主管協助緩緩出坑的態樣

Figure 259. Scene of worker goes out slowly with assist by chief of operation.

(五) 工地侷限空間作業緊急應變說明 Illustration of emergency response to confined space work at work site.

緊急應變應遵守事項

· 絕不進入缺氧危
　險作業場所救援
　（除非必要）

· 若已有妥善裝置
　（如吊升三腳架
　等），不需進入
　即可利用救生索
　救出罹災者。

圖 260　緊急應變應遵守事項

Figure 260. Items of obligation for emergency response.

圖 261　緊急應變人員所需的裝備及器材

Figure 261. Essential apparatus & equipment of rescue person for emergency response action.

5-7 營建工地熱危害的預防與對策 Precaution & strategy of heat hazard at construction site

　　因應全球暖化造成氣候異常變化，國內外氣溫偏高時有所聞，依據衛生福利部統計資料顯示，每年七至九月太陽照射強度及溫度較高時，發生熱疾病 (如：**熱中暑、熱衰竭、熱痙攣及熱暈厥⋯⋯等**) 的**案例也較高**。對於經常性於室外作業，如營建作業、馬路修護、電線桿維修或從事農事等勞動者，尤需提高警覺及強化相關預防措施。再者，諸如環境風速、空氣溫度、溼度、輻射熱、個人生理熱負荷、熱調節能力及其他外加熱壓力因子等，均為影響戶外作業勞工健康原因之一，為強化從事戶外作業勞工健康保障，預防高溫環境引起之熱疾病，雇主應參照政府相關機關訂定的熱危害預防相關規定辦理，減少勞動者於室外作業時發生熱危害的意外事故。

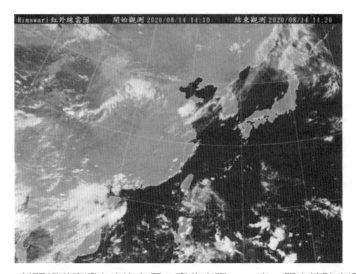

圖 262 新聞報導臺灣上空沒有雲！臺北出現 36.4 度 3 縣市慎防高溫傷害

Figure 262. According the medea's report that there was high temperature of 36.4F in Taipei area,peoples should prevent the harm of the sun.

一、何謂熱危害 What is heat illness

　　人體在熱環境工作，代謝產熱量與外在環境因素（氣溫、溼度、風速及輻射熱等）及衣著情形等共同作用，而造成身體產生熱負荷或熱蓄積情形，稱之為熱應力。因此，人體產生之種種生理現象稱為熱應變，如果這些應變導致健康之不良影響或破壞生理功能，則表示對生物體的熱危害。

圖 263 熱危害相關症狀關係圖

Figure 263. Diagram of heat illness in relational symptomes.

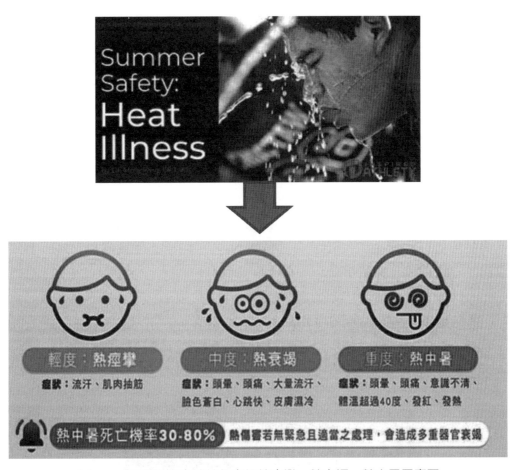

圖 264　夏季的安全談熱危害如熱痙攣、熱衰竭、熱中暑示意圖

Figure 264. Schematic diagram of heat illness in summer safety as heat cramps、heat exhaustion、heat stroke.

二、熱危害的類別 Classification of heat illness

(一) 熱痙攣 Heat cramps

　　熱痙攣症狀為身體不自主骨骼肌收縮所造成的肌肉疼痛，容易發生於大腿與肩部。通常在活動當中，或者是在長時間活動後休息時，大量流汗後補充開水或低張溶液卻未同步補充電解質時發生。水土不服或不適應的工作，有更高的機會發生熱痙攣。在病理學上，熱筋攣的發生是因為大量流汗導致身體肌肉鈉離子、鉀離子等電解質缺乏所造成。

(二) 熱衰竭 Heat exhaustion

　　造成熱衰竭的原因，可能是暴露在高溫的環境中或是過度運動後造成身體過度產熱。暴露於高溫環境或劇烈運動會導致身體水分或鹽分喪失，患者體溫可能正常或輕微上升。

熱衰竭和中暑的共通點是都是中心體溫上升，熱衰竭病人的中心體溫常會上升至38℃至40℃之間，常見的症狀包括：嚴重的不適感、口渴、噁心與嘔吐，熱衰竭一般會有輕微的脫水，有時伴隨著鈉離子不平衡的狀況；臨床上可能以高血鈉或低血鈉表現。相較於中暑，熱衰竭的患者一般不會有嚴重的神經系統症狀，因此神經系統症狀的有無可用來區分熱衰竭和中暑。

(三) 熱中暑 Heat stroke

患者體溫常會超過40.6℃且合併中樞神經症狀，如譫妄、抽搐或昏迷，中暑可分成傳統型中暑及勞動型中暑。

傳統型中暑：環境是造成此類中暑最重要的危險因子，這類型的中暑常發生在熱浪來襲、溫度上升時，個體暴露於高溫與高溼度的環境中，本身缺乏適應環境能力時，導致熱無法排出，就容易發生中暑的情形。

三、熱危害各類型的圖解說明 Illustration diagram was in various signs of heat illness.

(一) 熱痙攣的症狀 Symptom of heat cramps.

圖 265　熱痙攣症狀示意圖

Figure 265. Features of heat cramp.

(二) 熱痙攣的處置 Treatment of heat cramps.

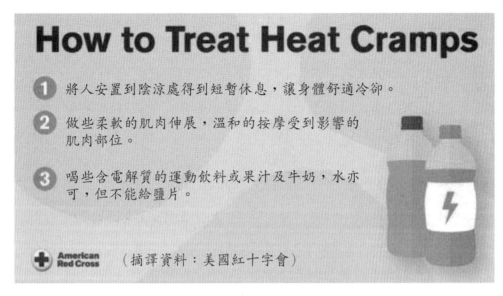

圖 266　熱痙攣症狀的處理要點

Figure 266. Key points of deal with to heat cramps symptom.

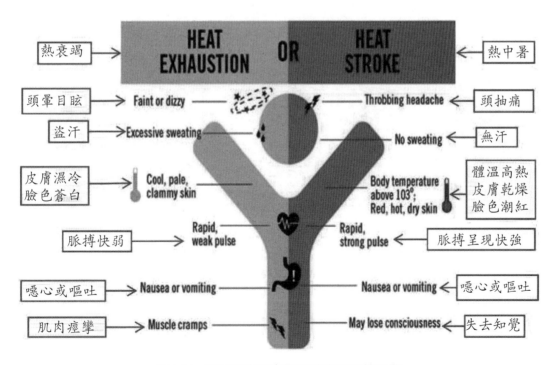

圖 267　如何判定熱衰竭及熱中暑的差異性

Figure 267. How identify as different of heat exhaustion & heat stroke.

圖 268　工地對工人引發熱衰竭或熱中暑的照護方式

Figure 268. The ways of treatment to workers who suffer with heat exhaustion & heat stroke at work site.

圖 269　熱危害的急救 5 步驟

Figure 269. There are five procedures of emergency treatment to heat illness.

四、職安衛法令相關規定 Regulations of occupation of safety & health acts.

為防範高氣溫環境引起之熱疾病，保障從事戶外作業勞工健康，雇主讓勞工於高氣溫環境下從事戶外作業時，應參考交通部中央氣象局發布之溫度及相對溼度資訊，採取下列危害預防及管理措施。

雇主於夏季期間使勞工從事戶外作業，應採取「降溫」、「飲水」、「休息」等預防措施參照（職業安全衛生設施規則第 324 條之 6），其中包括提供有遮蔽的休息區及適當飲水，使勞工適當補充水分與少許鹽分；同時避免勞工長時間從事高溫作業或視溫度高低調整工作與休息比例，減少熱暴露時間以維護勞工身心健康。

五、工地的熱危害防止管理與對策 Management & strategy of prevent the heat illness at site.

(一) 熱危害症狀的宣導及教育訓練課程 The symptom of heat illness & training courses has been propagandized at site.

圖 270 每日前集會向進場人員宣導防止熱危害的注意要點

Figure 270. Notices of heat illness that engineer declared to access workers in the daily assembly meeting.

圖 271　進場人員接受工務所安排有關熱危害防制的教育訓練態樣

Figure 271. Scene of workers as access at site who received the training of heat illness prevent that courses arranged with site office.

(二) 工區防制熱危害的相關設施與設備 Facilities & devices of heat illness prevent at work site.

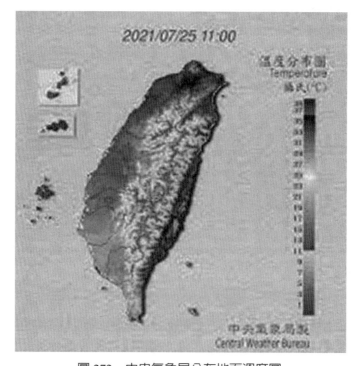

圖 272　中央氣象局公布地面溫度圖

Figure 272. Diagram of surface temperature was announced by Central Weather Bereau.

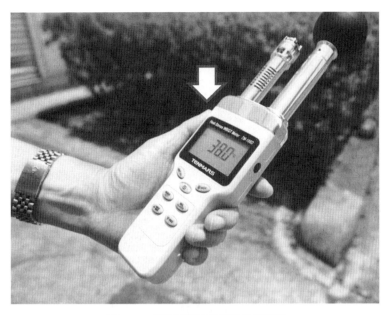

圖 273　工地購置的溫度感測器

Figure 273. Temperature sensor which purchased by site office.

圖 274　工地張貼有關熱危害相關訊息於明顯處

Figure 274. Related informations of heat illness & posters were post on apparent location at work site.

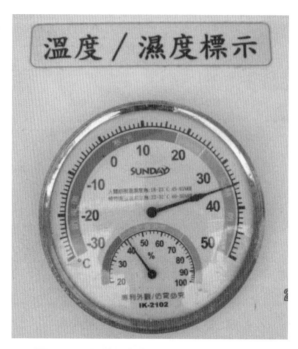

圖 275　溫溼度感測器被掛於工區明顯處

Figure 275. Sensor of temperature & humidity was hung on apparent location.

圖 276　工區設置作業人員休憩區的態樣

Figure 276. Rcreation area hase been planne for workers at site.

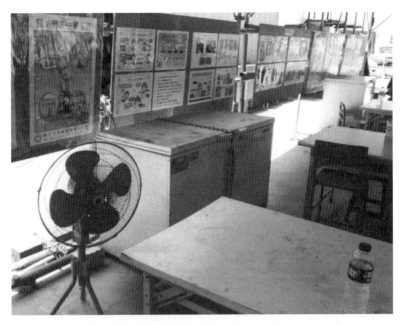

圖 277　休憩區擺設消暑設施，如冰櫃及電風扇等。

Figure 277. The relieving heat facilities of electrical fan &freezers were emplaced at recreation area.

圖 278　休憩區設置飲水機及其他預防中暑的附加物，如鹽、酸梅等。

Figure 278. Drinking water machine with salt & plums has been prepared at recreation area.

圖 279 工務所提供不同的漢方飲料給作業人員飲用

Figure 279. There are many herbs water in different taste which were supplied to workers using at recreation area.

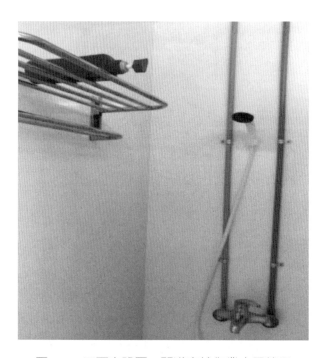

圖 280 工區內設置一間浴室給作業人員使用

Figure 280. There was one compartment of shower to workers using at work site.

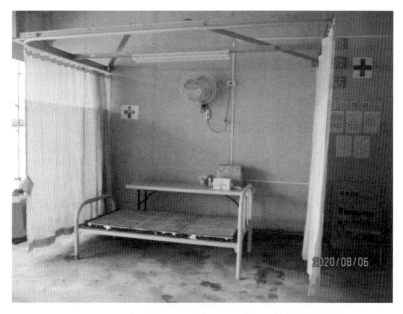

圖 281　工區內設置一間急救站及急救藥品等態樣

Figure 281. First Aid Station with first aid kit were prepared completely for workers using at work site.

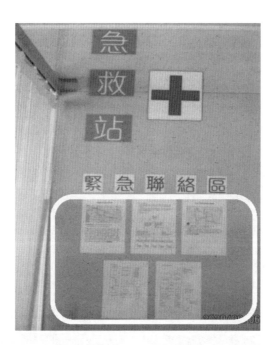

圖 282　緊急聯絡區電話，包括醫院、警消單位等。

Figure 282. The list of emergency telephone numbers was included the hospital、police station & fire engine station etc.

圖 283　水平支撐裝置灑水管提供下部結構作業區人員消暑

Figure 283. Water sprinkled to the work place of raft foundation which water supply facility has been install on the struts of substructure.

圖 284　樓板柱筋預留部分規劃設置灑水管，提供作業區人員消暑。

Figure 284. Sprinkling water pipe was installed in dowel of colum on the slab that relief heat to the work place.

圖 285 灑水管進行作動提供作業區人員消暑的態樣

Figure 285. Workers had relieving heat by the sprinkling water pipe in operation at work place.

圖 286 遮陽網張掛於樓板角落供鋼筋工休息用

Figure 286. Sun shade nets was spread &tighten on the corner of slab that workers could have to take arrest under the nets.

圖 287　遮陽網張掛於模板作業區，減少模板工受到熱危害的態樣。

Figure 287. Sun shade nets have been spread on the top of work place where protect the form workers to prevent the heat illness at site.

第六章　新建工程安全衛生實務管理精要作業 Crucial Operation of Safety & Health Management to New Construction Project

6-1　動土前作業要點 Essential work operation before the ceremony of ground breaking.

6-2　開工動土後工區規劃作業要點 Essential work planning & operation after ceremony of ground breaking & commence.

6-3　地下結構分項工程安全衛生規劃暨執行要點 Essential work planning & executed of safety &health for the variant work of substructures.

6-4　地上結構分項工程安全衛生規劃暨執行要點 Essential work planning & executed of safety & health for the variant work of superstructures.

6-5　建築鋼筋混凝土結構工程 Structure construction of architecture was reinforced concrete.

6-6　鋼骨鋼筋混凝土結構工程 Structure construction was steel reinforced concrete.

6-7　鋼骨結構工程 Steel structure construction.

6-8　創改型系統模板工程 Creation & improvement type of formwork system construction.

6-1 動土前作業要點 Essential work operation before the ceremony of ground breaking

場地履勘危害調查及評估作業 Hazard investigation & assess operation of work site survey.

(一) 基地位址 Site location

(二) 周邊環境 Related circumstance

(三) 地形及地質 Landforms & geology

(四) 地區天候 Weather of regionalism aera

(五) 道路系統 Road system

(六) 公共設施 Public supply facilities

(七) 醫療院所 Hospital & clinic

(八) 警消救援單位 Police station & fire brigade

(九) 建材支援性 Construction material supply

圖 288　新建工程場地履勘的態樣

Figure 288. Location of new construction project where was as the scene of site survey.

圖 289　公共設施（五大管線）址界試挖確認作業

Figure 289. Public utilities as electricity, water, gas, fire fighting, & telecommunication where have to dig to identify the location & scope.

6-2 開工動土後工區規劃作業要點 Essential work planning & operation after ceremony of ground breaking & commence

圖 290　新建工程準備動土典禮事宜的態樣

Figure 290. Affairs of ground-breaking ceremony was prepared for new construction project.

圖 291 　大鋼牙破碎機進行舊屋拆除作業的態樣

Figure 291. Old building was tore down with concrete buster which in progress of the work.

圖 292 　舊屋拆除後所有的廢鋼筋及殘料將被運棄的態樣

Figure 292. Debris of hoses as rebar & others has been deliveried with truck at site.

一、工區全方位配置規劃 Planning as all-domain of work site layout.

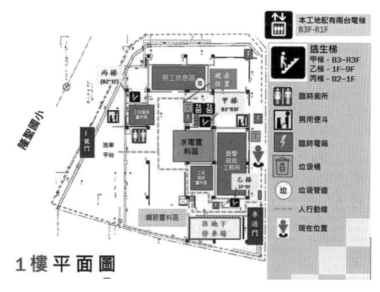

圖 293　工區範圍相關假設作業規劃配置執行

Figure 293. All related temporary works have been planed & execute at site.

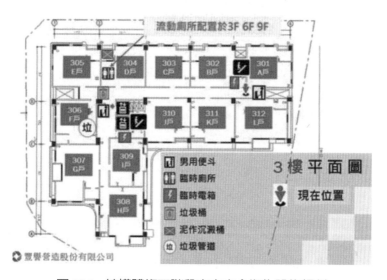

圖 294　結構體施工階段室內安全衛生設施規劃

Figure 294. All safety & health facilities have been planned & executed during the structure in progress at site.

二、工地圍籬組立 onstruction site hoardingerrected.

圖 295　工地圍籬綠化植栽及色彩創意呈現

Figure 295. Green plants with creative colors were appearance on the site hoarding.

圖 296　工地圍籬帆布彩印生動的臺灣蝴蝶美姿

Figure 296. Printed butterflies on the cavas which were spread tightly on the site hoarding. .

圖 297　工地圍籬於幹道路口交叉處需採鏤空圍籬

Figure 297. Hoarding panel as hollow were erected at corner of intersection at work site.

圖 298　工地進出動線大門可採分隔型式

Figure 298. Access gates of separate joined type were erected at work site.

圖 299　工地進出動線大門可採摺疊型式

Figure 299. Access gates of panel folding type were erected at work site.

圖 300　工地大門必須安裝車輛進出警示燈，以達安全示警作用。

Figure 300. For the safety in warning that warning light should mount aside the access gate.

圖 301 企業標章及安全標示旗幟可懸掛於工地明顯處

Figur301.Banner of enterprise & safety symbal flag were haung on the appropriate location at work site.

圖 302 風向袋的懸掛有利於工地吊掛作業的安全

Figur302. Windsocket was hung on at site that good for the hoisting operation in progressing as reference.

圖 303　工務所旁規劃開心花園可增加工作效率

Figure 303.Fun recreation of garden could ehence the efficience of the work where aside the site office.

圖 304　工務所屋頂必須有防颱的安全措施

Figure 304. The facilities of prevent the typhoon that essential part on the roof for safety.

圖 305　工務所的上下樓梯為安全考量應加裝背襯板

Figure 305. Stairs which should has lining plates on the back for safety concern.

圖 306　工務所設置急救設備、鞋櫃及滅火器等設施

Figure 306. There were first aid device、cabnets & fire extinguisher instlled st site office.

圖 307　廁所的照明、通風及清潔是必要條件

Figure 307. Toilet where requirement is good illumination, ventilation & tidy for sanitary.

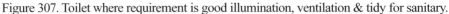

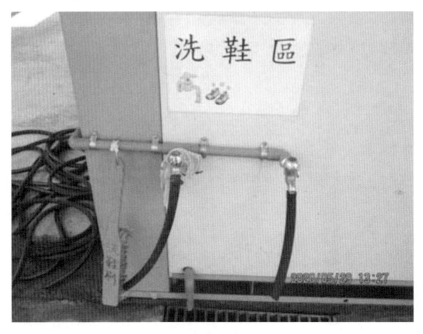

圖 308　工務所設置洗鞋區防止環境汙染

Figure 308. Shoes-washing location has been set up at site office where prevents the environment pollution.

圖 309　工務所設置手機充電區供作業人員使用

Figure 309. In-charge sockets are provided for cellar phone of workers at site office.

圖 310　工地的變壓器及室外分電盤均有臨時防護隔離設施

Figure 310. There are temporary protection & isolated facilities to transformer & temporary distribution panel at site.

圖 311 工地的漏電檢測器及綠色環保垃圾桶均備齊

Figure 311. Leakage detector & cans of green recycle were prepared completely at site.

圖 312 工地用硬鋪面作為洗車平台（內凹式）並設置洩水孔

Figure 312. Platform of vehicle washing as concrete had been set up with drain hole at work site.

圖 313　工地用型鋼＋角鋼作為洗車平台，需設置洩水孔及沉澱池。

Figure 313. Platform of vehicle washing as angle steel with H shape steel where attached drain hole & sediment pond.

圖 314　棄土卡車於洗車台沖洗輪胎後出場的態樣

Figure 314. Dump truck was washing the wheels by water jet on the platform.

圖 315　工地設置的作業人員休憩區態樣

Figure 315. Recreation zone has been engaged for workers at site.

圖 316　職安衛相關法令及安衛管理相關訊息均公布張貼

Figure 316. Acts of Safety & Health with safety management regulationswas post on the bulletum to add safety conception to workers.

圖 317 職災案例張貼於公布欄，以提升作業人員安全意識。

Figure 317. Cases of Occupational disaster were post on the bulletin to promote the safety conception of workers at site.

圖 318　進入工區的作業人員個人防護具需參照人形立牌穿戴完全

Figure 318. Workers who access into work site that they should refer the typical personal protective equipment of diagram poster sign board, are permitted with securiety person.

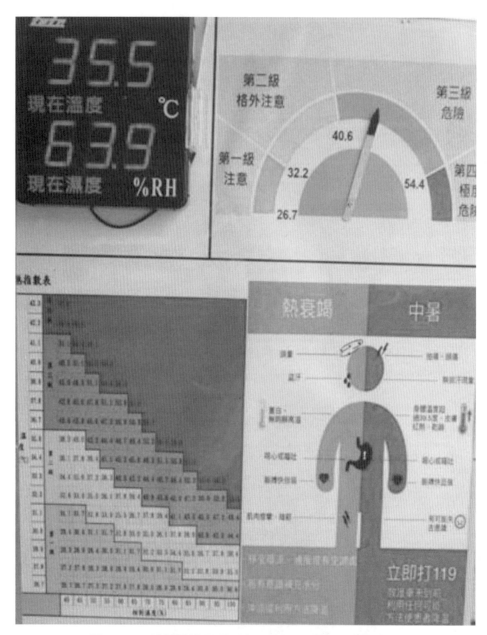

圖 319　工地提供當日溫溼度及防止熱危害的相關資訊

Figure 319. Sensor of temperature & humidity of daily was hung on apparent location with related information of prevent the heat illness.

圖 320　工地針對特種流行疾病加強宣導及防制

Figure 320. Information of special disease & epidemic as covid-19 which diagrams were post on the apparent location to propaganda & prevent.

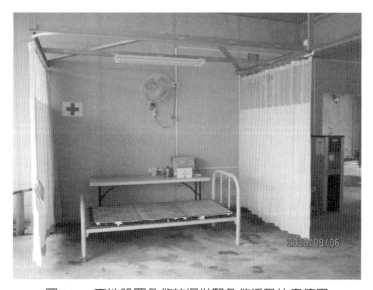

圖 321　工地設置急救站提供緊急救援及休息使用

Figure 321. First-aid station was set up at site where provide the emergency rescue & take a rest to workers who neeeded.

6-3 地下結構分項工程安全衛生規劃暨執行要點 Essential work planning & executed of safety & health for the sectoral work of substructures.

一、基樁工程概述 Summary of pile construction.

　　樁基礎是由若干個沉入土中的單樁，通過頂部的承台或樑聯繫起來的一種基礎。它的作用是將淺層土層難以承受的上部荷載，傳遞到深處承載力較大的土層或岩層上，或將上部軟弱持力層擠密，以提高地基的密實度，進而使地基的承載力大幅度提高。然而基樁的機具和功能也是多樣化，因應地形及作業環境的條件，專業承商也會慎重選擇機具及工法。

　　新建工程如基地在一些區域，如山坡地或施工動線較狹窄區域，採用大型鑽機無法有充足之動線，致使無法施工，則可採用臺灣特有改裝挖土機而成之 PC400 或 PC200 鑽掘機，其機動性及施工性較佳。然而因各種地質條件不一及品質要求標準不同，一般而言，改裝挖土機成本最低，如使用 AUGER 鑽機則機動性較大，因成本較高，但其高效率的特性，爲業界最常用的施工方法。

　　排樁因地層回填層或較軟地層較厚時，則需將薄套管下至不會坍塌之深度，而下套管之方式，則需仰賴震動機將套管震至不坍之深度。接著採用鑽機進行鑽掘施工，鑽掘之順序需採跳樁施工，以免影響已完成澆置樁體在未凝結時因土層解壓而產生裂縫及破壞；接續以超音波檢測儀或紅外線垂測儀檢測鑽孔垂直度，鑽孔完成之注漿方式，因採用之注漿材料不同而有兩種處理方式，若採用水泥砂漿（預壘樁），則先行注漿完成後，再吊放鋼筋籠或型鋼；而若採混凝土爲注漿材時，則需先行吊放鋼筋籠完成後，再採用特密管進行混凝土澆置。

　　其間因注漿材質之不同，而需考量鑽孔因等候混凝土之送料時間是否會坍塌，如果會塌，則需採鑽孔前先行下套管之施作方式。於排樁注漿材灌注完成後，待 7 天後需進行將排樁頂開挖，以利樁頭打除，待清潔完成即進行兩側模組繫樑鋼筋之綁紮，完成檢查後，即可進行繫樑混凝土之澆注。本章逐將詳細說明營建工程常用的基樁作業機具及不同的作業工法，施工期間有關現場安全衛生管理應注意事項，以防止任何災害的發生。

(一) 鑽掘式擋土排樁 (AUGER 鑽機) 作業，安全衛生管理的關鍵要領 Crucial skill of safety & health management for bored piling work as retaining campshed by auger drill rig machine

圖 322　工區鑽掘機駛進樁位點準備鑽掘作業的態樣

Figure 322. Auger bored piling machine approached the pile location to had the bored piles in progress.

圖 323　工區進行鑽掘作業的區域要有臨時防護設施

Figure 323. There was temporary protective facilities around the working area of auger bored piling machine which was in progressing.

圖 324　作業主管指揮鑽掘螺旋取土筒緩緩進入套筒的態樣

Figure 324. Chief of work gestured the auger drill with soil bucket into the casin.

圖 325　鑽掘螺旋取土筒提升鬆開封鈑並左右擺動，將筒內原土甩出。

Figure 325. Soil of soil bucket was thrown out with swung of soil bucket which rose up aside & loosen the sealed plate.

圖 326　現場吊架及鋼索必須於作業前執行檢點

Figure 326. Hoisting hanger with steel wire rope which should be inspected prior the operation.

圖 327　鋼筋籠吊掛作業迴旋區域不得有作業人員暫留

Figure 327. Steel cage was raised by a hoist which has no workers to stay in the radius of round.

圖 328　基樁進行混凝土澆置時，輸送管需有穩定索防止擺動。

Figure 328. When pile in concrete pouring work that pipe line should be tied tight to prevent the pipe in swing.

圖 329　每月定期檢查現場的鋼索，如符合安全規定，則依每月色標噴漆識別。

Figure 329. Cable wires are inspected on regular in every month that are sprayed the color as mark on cable wires which in accordance with the safety regulation.

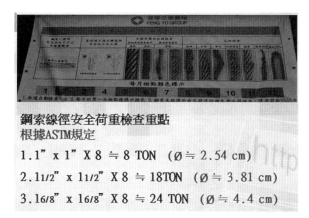

圖 330　色標管理：鋼索經檢查合格後，依當月顏色噴漆作為安全辨識。

Figure 330. Color code which means that cable wire is inspected in regular of per month as safety identification by different color spray on it.

＊ 現場作業前執行作業檢點暨缺失改善

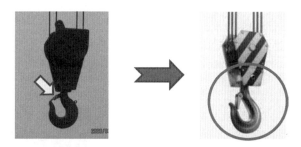

圖 331　起重機吊勾的防滑舌片必須比照右圖的標準模式

Figure 331. Gravity safety latch on a sling hook was utilized on the right position as refer the right picture.

圖 332　工地使用柴油發電機前，必須做好銅棒接地系統（圈起處）。

Figure 332. Copper rod of grounding was inserted on the earth prior the operation of diesel fuel generater.

(二)預壘樁作業，安全衛生管理的關鍵要領 Crucial skill of safety & health management for pre packed piling work as retaining campshed by auger machine

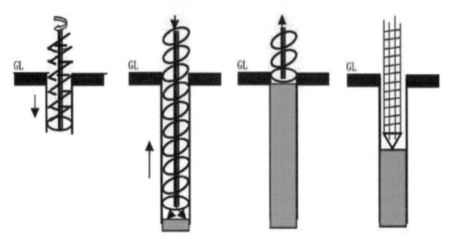

1. 螺旋鑽桿鑽孔　2. 逐次提升鑽桿　3. 砂漿灌注完成　4. 置入鋼筋籠

圖 333　預壘樁施工作業流程圖示

Figure 333. The diagram of pre packed pile operation.

圖 334　預壘樁施工機具進場整備作業態樣

Figure 334. Scene of all mechanisms of pre packed pile have been delivered & maintenance at work site.

圖 335　螺旋鑽進行鑽掘作業態樣

Figure 335. Drill of bored pile which operated in progressing at site.

圖 336　工地現場工人製作鋼筋籠的態樣

Figure 336. Rebar cages have been made with workers at work site.

圖 337　鑽掘作業與製作鋼筋籠同步進行的態樣

Figure 337. Scene of boring operation & rebar cages were synchronized at site.

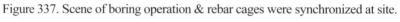

圖 338　水泥砂漿經由幫浦壓送，經由中空鑽桿注入樁體內部。

Figure 338. Mortar was delivered into the pile through by the central hollow pipe of drill with the dynamic pump.

圖 339　螺旋中空鑽桿放置於作業現場準備維修

Figure 339. Hollow shaft were layed on the ground for maintenance.

圖 340　鋼筋籠準備吊放進入已注滿水泥砂漿的樁內

Figure 340. Rebar cage was hoisted with crane that rebar cage was plugin slowly into the pile where full pour the mortar.

圖 341　預壘樁施工完成的態樣

Figure 341. Scene of pre packed piles which were completion at site.

＊ 現場作業前執行作業檢點暨缺失改善

圖 342　單線不得與插頭刃片相互交接，應採用防水型插座。

Figure 342. Power cord can't connect the plug with isolative tape on the contrary that it should use the socket of water proof.

圖 343　發電機的用電設備必須要有完整的保護罩

Figure 343. Protective shield mounted on the exterior of power supply device of diesel-electric set.

(三) 場鑄樁作業，安全衛生管理的關鍵要領 Crucial skill of safety & health management for cast in place piling work as retaining campshed by auger machine.

圖 344　場鑄樁位置經測量定位後及埋入鋼管的態樣

Figure 344. Fixed position of pile after survey measure where insert the steel sleeving.

圖 345　工地螺旋式鑽掘機進行旋鑽作業的態樣

Figure 345. Scene of the auger was in progressing to boiling piles at site.

圖 346　鑽桿旋鑽至設計深度進行起桿及停止作業的態樣

Figure 346. Auger drilled down to the design depth that auger should rise up to finished the work.

圖 347　鑽桿進行左右迴旋，將葉片上原土甩出的態樣。

Figure 347. Soil on the metal attached to handle on the twisted rod was thrown out to the ground at site.

圖 348　螺旋鑽桿使用固定軛架在鋼管上，表示鑽掘深度已完成。

Figure 348. Auger rods were hung on the steel sleeving which boring piles have been completed.

圖 349　作業人員正在製作鋼筋籠的態樣

Figure 349. Rebar cages were manufactured with workers at site.

圖 350　鋼筋籠被吊放入樁的態樣

Figure 350. Scene of rebar cage was hoisted with crane into the bored pile at site.

圖 351　鋼筋籠被吊放至樁內且定位於設計的高程

Figure 351. Rebar cage was hosted into the bored pile & fixed to the designed elevation.

圖 352　作業人員於現場利用混凝土壓送管的管夾進行接續作業

Figure 352. Concrete workers were to connect the pipes in together with clips at site.

圖 353　場鑄基樁澆置混凝土完成及鋼管拔出後的態樣

Figure 353. Scene of the bored pile which after concrete had grouted in completion & steel sleeve had been pull outby crane at site.

圖 354　打除場鑄基樁樁頭劣質混凝土後，進行繫樑的混凝土作業。

Figure 354. The top of cast-in-place piles which bastard concrete was break down for the concrete work of connection girder.

＊ 現場作業前執行作業檢點暨缺失改善

圖 355　甩清鑽桿原土時，造成塵土飛揚的態樣。

Figure 355. soil was thrown out from the auger that was as dust float in the air.

圖 356　葉子表面沾黏塵土是鑽桿甩土所造成的

Figure 356. Surface of leaves were polluted of dust due to the soil was thrown with the auger.

圖 357　鑽掘作業區範圍需張掛防塵網，防止塵土飄散。

Figure 357. Net of dust prevention should be spread aside the boring work place to prevent the dust float everywhere.

(四) 衝擊樁作業，安全衛生管理的關鍵要領 Crucial skill of safety & health management for cast in place piling work of percussion hammer

圖 358　衝擊樁機器進場整備作業的態樣

Figure 358. Machine of percussion was delieveried at work place to preparation & maintenance.

圖 359　工程師進行全區衝擊樁樁位的量測態樣

Figure 359. Engineer conducted the survey & stake out the location of percussion hammer pile at work site.

圖 360　衝擊樁經測量定位後，即用螺旋鑽鑽孔的態樣。

Figure 360. Fixed position of pile after survey measure where left the auger as mark.

圖 361　樁位確定後，鋼管先安放以利後續樁錘作業。

Figure 361. Location of pile has been fix that stel sleeve has been placed to good for follow up work.

圖 362　工地單人操作往復式衝擊樁機器作業態樣

Figure 362. One worker operated the percussion drilling machine as reciprocating motion at site.

圖 363　衝擊樁達到設計深度後，工人使用取水筒將樁內泥水清出態樣。

Figure 363. When pile reached the designed depth that worker used the steel jug to pour the mud water out to the ground.

圖 364　工人於現場製作鋼筋籠的態樣

Figure 364. Steel cages have been erected & tied with workers at site.

圖 365　怪手將鋼筋籠吊升移位到已達設計深度的樁孔內置放

Figure 365. Steel cage has been hoisted & replaced into the inner of the pile with backhoe.

圖 366　怪手將特密管吊升移位到樁孔內已置放鋼筋籠的中間

Figure 366. Tremie pipe has been hoisted to the middle of the steel cage which was inner of the pile.

圖 367　混凝土材料藉由特密管將樁全部注滿的態樣

Figure 367. Concrete was grouting into the pile which was top off with tremie pipe.

二、開挖擋土支撐工程概述 Summary of retaining wall with strut & excavation construction

　　開挖擋土支撐工程包括擋土壁及支撐系統，此外，視工程需要，另外需規劃安全觀測系統、抽水系統、鄰房保護措施及地質改良等。基本上執行這些措施的目的，係爲維持開挖作業的穩定及鄰房的安全性。

擋土壁就營建工程而言，常用的工法有：

1. **兵樁工法**：其所用的鋼材有**鋼軌樁**、**H 型鋼**及 **I 型鋼**，而以鋼軌樁及 H 型鋼最爲常用。型鋼常用於一般性砂質或黏土質地盤，型鋼的尺寸及相關性質可參考一般鋼結構的書籍。鋼軌樁由於斷面較小，較容易貫入地盤，因此常用於較硬的地盤或卵礫石地盤，爲國內較常用之材料。視現地土壤性質及強度特性，兵樁之間均放置橫板條。

2. **鋼版樁工法**：爲將鋼版樁打入土中，並使之嵌合在一起的擋土工法。

3. **排樁工法的種類**：

3.1. **預疊樁**：預疊樁又稱爲 PIP 樁（Packed In Place pile），係利用螺旋鑽挖至預定深度後，緩慢提升鑽頭，同時由前端灌注預疊砂漿，以擠出土砂；灌漿完後，插入鋼筋籠或 H 型鋼。

3.2. **鋼筋混凝土樁**：挖孔的方式是利用機械挖孔至預定深度後，插入鋼筋籠，然後利用特密管灌注混凝土。

3.3. **連續壁又稱爲泥漿牆**：其工法係利用挖斗式 Masago 型挖掘機挖掘連續壁槽溝；挖掘

機具係利用鋼製抓斗之爪牙嵌鑿土石，並納入抓斗內，然後將抓斗提出槽外卸碴，無須將穩定液泵出槽外，免除處理泥漿分離設備，為操作相當簡易之工法。

連續壁體構築時，先依適合施工條件的長度予以分割成若干單元，每一個單元的施工，包括導牆施作、槽溝挖掘及混凝土澆鑄等階段。槽溝挖掘階段包括槽溝挖掘、淤泥清除（底部疏濬）及鋼筋籠吊放等過程；混凝土澆鑄階段則是槽溝單元之最後施作階段，乃是利用特密管工法將混凝土澆置於槽溝內而形成連續壁單元壁體。

3.4. **地錨開挖工法**：是用地錨取代支撐，以支承擋土壁側向力的作法。

(一)**鋼軌樁及水平支撐開挖作業，安全衛生管理的關鍵要領** Crucial skill of safety & health management for soldier piling & strut excavation work.

1. **鋼軌樁作業** Rail steel operation.

圖 368　現場鋼軌樁依放樣定位進行植入的態樣

Figure 368. Rail steel was press down into the earth at setting out with static driving machine.

圖 369　現場監視人員進行鋼軌樁垂直度及深度的觀測態樣

Figure 369. Worker as observer was watching the verticality & depth of rail steel which press down by machine.

圖 370　鋼軌樁被打設到設計深度完成的態樣

Figure 370. Scene of the rail steel which has been press down the earth comply with the design required.

圖 371　鋼軌樁進行橫擋（圍令）架設的態樣

Figure 371. Scene of waling were mounted on the rail steel for strut work.

圖 372　鋼軌樁的繫樑及嵌放橫板條完成的態樣

Figure 372. Completion of planks was lagging between the two rail steel with tie beam.

2. 水平支撐開挖作業 Strut & excavation operation

圖 373　現場水平支撐進行吊掛組裝的態樣

Figure 373. Scene of strut components was hoisting to assemble together at site.

圖 374　現場水平支撐作業範圍需設置安全護欄防止人員墜落

Figure 374. Guard rail should be erected around the scope of strut to prevent the fall accident.

圖 375 現場水平支撐短向比長向先行架設的態樣

Figure 375. Scene of the strut components in short side were assembled prior to long side.

3. 作業區安全衛生管理的要點 Major points of safety & health management which excuteded at site.

圖 376 作業主管要求現場作業人員均需配戴背負式安全帶作業

Figure 376. Superior ordered all workers that they should wear the harness to assemble the work of strut at site.

圖 377　材料進場占用道路作業需派交通指揮人員疏散車流

Figure 377. Traffic conducter has the scatter to vehicles when the materials of truck stop aside the main road.

(二) H 型鋼樁作業，安全衛生管理的關鍵要領 Crucial skill of safety & health management for the work of H type steel piling.

1. H 型鋼樁作業 H type steel piling operation

圖 378　工地 H 型鋼材料進場及整備作業

Figure 378. H type steel has been approached & preparedness at site.

圖 379　工地振動液壓打樁機正夾住 H 型鋼作業態樣

Figure 379. H type steel was clipped by vibratory hydraulic driver in progressing.

圖 380　作業人員比手勢將 H 型鋼定位作業態樣

Figure 380. Worker who gave the gesture to operater that they pitched the H type steel at right position.

圖 381　工地振動液壓打樁機開始作業的態樣

Figure 381. H type steel was pitched & driving with vibratory hydaulic driver at site.

圖 382　H 型鋼依照樁的位置，依序被植入到預定的深度。

Figure 382. H type steel was driven into in sequence at right position & designed depth with vibratory hydraulic driver.

圖 383　H 型鋼樁之間的空隙，均嵌入橫板條作為擋土的態樣。

Figure 383. Boards were lagged between the H type steel for retaining.

圖 384　工地 H 型鋼樁及橫板條施作完成的態樣

Figure 384. Scene of king pile with lagging was completed at site.

2. 水平支撐開挖作業 Strut & excavation operation

圖 385　工區部分區域已完成中間柱的態樣

Figure 385. Scene of the center posts were inserted completely by vibratory hydraulic driver of some area at site.

圖 386　現場振動液壓打樁機繼續施打中間柱的態樣

Figure 386. Center post was driven with vibratory drawl driver at site.

圖 387　第一層的水平支撐進行吊掛及組裝的態樣

Figure 387. Scene of first layer ranking strut has been hoisted & assembled at site.

圖 388　水平支撐及開挖作業範圍已完成安全護欄組立的態樣

Figure 388. Guard rail was erected completely around the strut working area.

3. 作業區安全衛生管理的要點 Major points of safety & health management which excuteded at site.

圖 389 第一層的水平支撐完成後，必須在長短不同方向安置安全母索。

Figure 389. Horizontal life line should be mounted on the center post in two different sides of (L/ S) on the strut scope.

圖 390 現場進行土方開挖作業時，需有作業主管在場監視。

Figure 390. Supervisor should observe the excavation work in progressing at site.

圖 391　圍令與 H 型鋼樁之間的空隙需用混凝土填滿

Figure 391. Plain concrete should grout into the space between the waling and king pile.

圖 392　工區臨時土方堆置需用防塵網覆蓋，防止空汙發生。

Figure 392. Excavated soil waste was temporary deposited at site which should spread the net to prevent the air pollution arise.

(三)鋼板樁作業，安全衛生管理的關鍵要領 Safety & health management as crucial skill of sheet pile work.

1. 鋼板樁作業 sheet pile operation

圖 393　鋼板樁作業機具及材料進場整備的態樣

Figure 393. Machines & materials were approached & preparedness at work site.

圖 394　工程師正監視鋼板樁植入作業的態樣

Figure 394. Engineer who observed the sheet pile which was driven with vibratory hydraulic driven at site.

圖 395　工程師與作業主管正量測鋼板樁植入的深度

Figure 395. Engineer and supervisor that they measured the length from the top of sheet pile in together.

圖 396　工作人員定住鋼板樁進行鎖口穿料接鈑的作業

Figure 396. worker pitched and was threading the sheet pile into a panel at site.

2. 水平支撐開挖作業 Strut & excavation operation

圖 397　鋼板樁打設封合完成作業的態樣

Figure 397. Scene of the sheet piles was driven into a panel in complication.

圖 398　螺旋鑽機進場進行中間柱植入引孔鑽掘作業

Figure 398. The lead hole was driven with the auger drilling machine to center post was inserted in.

圖 399　中間柱被植入引孔處完成作業的態樣

Figure 399. Scene of center post has been driven into the lead hole in completion.

圖 400　工程師現場監督開挖區臨時動線鐵板鋪設作業

Figure 400. Engineer paid attention & instructed that temporary access way where placing the steel plates for excavational zone.

圖 401　棄土卡車及怪手均於施工構台進行開挖作業

Figure 401. Dump trucks & backhoe were in progressing to excavated work at site.

圖 402　第一層的水平支撐完成後，即進行下一階段開挖作業。

Figure 402. There is excavation work on going after first layer strut should be completed at site.

3. 作業區安全衛生管理的要點 Major points of safety & health management which excuteded at site.

圖 403　工區作業人員進入開挖區的上下設備需設置扶手

Figure 403. Stair case with hand rails of excavation zone should be mounted to convenience of workers at site.

圖 404　工區內材料吊掛進行搬運，也要採二點安全吊掛規定。

Figure 404. Materials was delivered to another place for deposition that is must to hoist in two hanging points comply with the act & safety regulation at site.

(四) 擋土排樁作業，安全衛生管理的關鍵要領 Crucial skill of safety & health management for the work of retaining campshed

1. 山坡地擋土排樁水平支撐作業 The strut work of retain campshedat hillside.

圖 405　規劃動線的土石挖除，以利擋土排樁水平支撐作業。

Figure 405. Plan of access way where soil & cobble should be removed todump that was good for the strut of retains campshed work.

圖 406　怪手剷除擋土排樁內側的原土，將其裸露出來。

Figure 406. Scene of retain campshed where interior soil was digging out with backhoe to exposed the appearance.

圖 407　螺旋鑽機進場引孔鑽掘完成後，中間柱植入引孔內部的態樣。

Figure 407. The lead hole was driven with the auger drill shaft to center post that was inserted inside the hole.

2. 水平支撐開挖作業 Strut & excavation operation

圖 408　部分範圍的中間柱植入完成後，支撐鋼材陸續進場的態樣。

Figure 408. Components of strut was approached to work site when center posts was erected completely in the site.

圖 409　基於安全考量，部分中間柱底部施以灌注混凝土加固作業。

Figure 409. For the sake of safety that some of center post should has grounted concrete into the bottom for stiffness.

圖 410　擋土排樁與第一層水平支撐接合的態樣

Figure 410. Scene of retain campshed which connected the strut in first layer.

圖 411　開挖土石陸續運棄是配合水平支撐組立作業

Figure 411. Excavated material was deliveried out by dump truck that the operation just matching up the work of strut operation.

圖 412　技師檢視擋土排樁上的化錨鋼筋及圍令之支撐三角架安全的態樣

Figure 412. Registered engineer checked the anchor bolts of retain campshed & triangle brackets for waling as stiff which comply the safety regulation.

圖 413　擋土排樁上的化錨鋼筋及圍令使用電焊焊接以加強勁度

Figure 413. Anchor bolts of retain campshed were welding with the wales for the stiff enforce.

圖 414　基於安全考量，擋土排樁外側的側壓力逐圍令增加一層加勁的態樣。

Figure 414. Considering of safety that two layers of waling which were stacked together to reinforce the strength for strut to against the lateral compression of retain campshed.

圖 415　現場澆注混凝土將圍令和擋土排樁的間隙填實之態樣。

Figure 415. Scene of the pouring concrete into the gap where between the waling & retain campshed.

圖 416　擋土排樁與四種不同高程的水平支撐接合之態樣

Figure 416. Scene of the strut which was errrected & assemblied in four different elevation with the retain campshed at site.

圖 417　現場開挖擋土及支撐三合一作業其壯觀的鳥瞰照

Figure 417. Picture of bird's eye view performed the spectacular of excavation, retain campshed & steel strut works which as called 3 in 1.

3. 作業區安全衛生管理的要點 Major points of safety & health management which excuteded at work site.

圖 418　移動式起重機翻倒的主要原因：a. 吊重超過額定荷重；b. 外伸撐座底部需鋪設鐵板或墊材防止沉陷

Figure 418. Mobile crane was overturn in operation which major causes: a. weight of lifting over the rated load, b. extention outrigger which bottom shall place the steel plate or timbers stack together to prevent the outrigger to sink.

圖 419　工地吊掛作業前的檢點重要事項：a. 作業範圍的臨時防護設置；b. 前後的油壓撐座需有墊木及完全伸展

Figure 419. There was some check points prior the hanging operation at site: a. that the protective facilities as guard rail must be installed completely. b. outrigger in four sets should extend completely which bottom of outriggers that must be placed the mats or timbers stacking in togethers.

(五)連續壁作業，安全衛生管理的關鍵要領 Safety & health management as crucial skill of diaphragm wall work.

1. 連續壁作業，Diaphragm wall operation

圖 420　工區導牆位置進行開挖的態樣

Figure 420. The location of guide wall where excavated in progresss.

圖 421　工區導牆進行混凝土作業

Figure 421. There was concrete work of guide wall which on going at site.

圖 422　導牆混凝土作業施作完成的態樣

Figure 422. Scene of the guide wall was finished the concrete work.

圖 423　導牆相關範圍均澆注混凝土作為鋪面的態樣

Figure 423. Placing the concrete to related place where adjacent the guide wall for pavement.

圖 424　導牆完成後，需用杉木對撐以防止傾斜狀態發生。

Figure 424. To prevented the oblique appearance that it had to use the round timber to bracing the guide wall.

圖 425　導牆完成後，為防止人員墜落意外需用全覆蓋防護。

Figure 425. Guide wall should be covered completely to prevent the fall accident.

圖 426　油壓式蛤型抓斗（MASAGO）於槽溝進行抓掘作業的態樣

Figure 426. Scene of MASAGO hydraulic long bucket method was operating in the trench at site.

圖 427　蛤型抓斗內的原土被吊至棄土桶上方丟棄

Figure 427. Soil was grabbed into the clam shell bucket that ascent to throw soil away into the waste soil tank.

圖 428　鋼筋工及電焊工正在製造連續壁鋼筋籠

Figure 428. Steel reinforciement cage was fabricated by welders & workers rebar tying at site.

圖 429　鋼筋籠完成後，吊掛點、鋼索和索具均需落實檢點作業。

Figure 429. Before steel cage was hoistng by cable wire, hoisting point & lifting gears that must be examined with visual prior operation after steel cage was fabricated at site.

圖 430　鋼筋籠起吊後，於適當高度暫停檢視吊掛物有無異狀發生。

Figure 430. When steel cage was hoisting on the height of several meters that suspended a while to sbserved the abnormal condition be happened

圖 431　電焊工進行鋼筋籠搭接的態樣

Figure 431. Steel cage which rebar's overlap must be welded together for two different panel units with the arc welding machine by welder.

圖 432　鋼筋籠搭接完成後，緩緩下降到預定深度的態樣。

Figure 432. Steel cage which hoisted & lift slowly into the trench to the scheduled depth after the rebar's overlap has been welded completely.

圖 433　現場用扁鐵清刷公單元與完成單元的端鈑介面殘餘淤泥

Figure 433. Flat iron was lift to the trench as up & down motion to cleaned the residual mud in the gap of join two different diaphragm wall.

圖 434　特密管已被放置於鋼筋籠中間準備進行混凝土澆置

Figure 434. Tremie was put in the middle for concrete pouring to the steel cage.

2. 開挖和水平支撐作業 Excavation & strut operation

圖 435　連續壁劣質打除後，圍令三角架安裝的態樣。

Figure 435. Scene of top diaphragm wall where was poor quality concrete that must be gotten rid &
triangle brackets were mounted on the side for the waling installation of strut.

圖 436 中間柱植入完成後，部分支撐鋼材已陸續進場的態樣。

Figure 436. Components of strut was approached to work site that center posthas been inserted completely at strut zone.

圖 437 開挖至適當的深度，第一層水平支撐進行架設作業。

Figure 437. Started the installation of strut in first layer which excavation of backhoe to dug on the proper depth after measured.

圖 438　工地進行水平支撐架設必須設置合格的上下設備

Figure 438. Staircases with handrails should be mounted at appropriate locationthat the strut was in progressing.

圖 439　界臨水平支撐的施工構台需設置標準安全護欄

Figure 439. The guard rail should erected around onto the deck where adjacent the strut zone.

圖 440　施工構台安全護欄底部設置型鋼輪擋，防止營建機具有翻落之虞。

Figure 440. Installed the wheel barricades on the bottom of guardrail around the deck that was to prevent the overturn accident with truck & construction machines.

圖 441　水平支撐範圍必須設置安全通道及上下設備

Figure 441. Planned & installed the safety access & staircase on the struc zone of underground construction.

圖 442 施工構台下方的中間柱焊接角鋼斜撐，以防止挫曲發生。

Figure 442. To prevented the buckling of center post that used the angle steels as cross welded on the center post where beneath the deck zone.

圖 443 伸縮臂挖土機於施工構台進行深開挖作業態樣

Figure 443. There was two flexible boom of clam shell were working to dig the soil on the deck from the underground.

3. 連續壁暨水平支撐開挖作業安全衛生管理的要點

圖 444　水平支撐材料進場需採兩點吊掛作業

Figure 444. Materials of strut work which approached & hoist was in progress should have two hanging points to hanger.

圖 445　施工構台未設置安全護欄，恐有人員墜落之虞。

Figure 445. Decks has been installed completely of strut work that guard rails must be erected to prevent the fall accident.

圖 446　施工構台拆卸安全護欄進行開挖作業需有作業主管在場監督

Figure 446. Supervisor of excavation work who should observe at site when the guard rails were removed temporary to excavation work.

圖 447　水平支撐範圍設置的安全母索需定期檢查

Figure 447. The rod with the life line which should has periodic safety inspection to the waling & strut scope.

圖 448　連續壁體樑的預留筋翹起部分應改善，防止人員受傷。

Figure 448. Dowels of beam on the diaphragm wall that has some of rebar up turn which should bend down to prevent workers got injury.

圖 449　連續壁鋼筋籠要吊掛前，作業人員必須檢查以防止鋼筋飛落。

Figure 449. It was essential work to check the elements of steel cage with workers which might cause falling disaster prior the steel cage in hoisting operation.

圖 450　電焊機負載側的正負端子都必須絕緣包覆防止感電意外

Figure 450. To prevent the shock accident that terminal of positive / negative connected the crimping terminals of power cables that should be wraped to isolated with materials of AC arc welding machine.

圖 451　柴油發電機必須有接地銅棒設置

Figure 451. It is required to grounding rod that plugin the earth with device of diesel oil generator.

圖 452　工地所使用的吊掛索具及鋼索，均依每月色標管理進行檢查及噴漆。

Figure 452. Cable wires & lifting gears should be inspected one time on the last date in a month that spray the different color according the colour code on the cable wire which comply the safety regulation at site.

圖 453　洗車台沉澱池的沉泥需定期清理及運棄

Figure 453. The mud has been cleaned & dump to the sedimentation tank with truck on regular.

圖 454　連續壁抓掘作業期間，需派員不定時清洗地面以防意外事件發生。

Figure 454. To prevent the accident occurred that worker should execute the tidy work as spray water to cleaned the slurry & mud on the ground during the duration of diaphragm wall operation.

(六) 背拉式地錨作業，安全衛生管理的關鍵要領 Safety & health management as crucial skill of tieback anchors.

圖 455　工地振動液壓打樁機開始植入 H 型鋼作業的態樣

Figure 455. Scene of H type steel was pitched & driving with vibratory hydaudic driver at site.

圖 456　工地先行打設 H 型鋼於開挖及地錨作業交界範圍的態樣

Figure 456. There was the primary work of H type steel which drove in the adjacent location of the work in excavation & ground anchor.

圖 457　工地 H 型鋼樁及橫板條施作完成後，即進行第一階開挖的態樣。

Figure 457. Scene of king pile with lagging was completed then follow up work of excavation was in progressing at site.

圖 458　履帶式地錨鑽堡機進場進行第一段鑽掘引孔作業

Figure 458. Caterpillar drilling machine of ground anchor accessed the site to ready for drilling work.

圖 459　作業人員依照設計長度進行鋼鍵組裝

Figure 459. Workers fabricated the strand tendons according to the fixed on charge length which were identification at site.

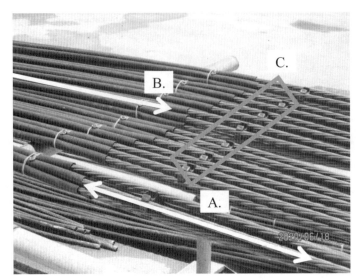

圖 460　鋼鍵長度可分前段叫錨碇段（A.），後段叫自由段（B.）及鋼鍵環型夾片（C.）

Figure 460. Strand tendon was divided two different parts that one part is called unbounded of free length (as white arrow),the other is called bonded of fixed length (as yellow arrow)that tendons were bound in together as a bundle with loop(as red frame).

3. 地錨鑽孔作業 Ground anchore drilling work.

圖 461　鑽堡機依照設計孔徑、深度、角度進行旋轉及衝擊完成引孔的態樣

Figure 461. Borehole which diameter, depth & anger degree were comply with design's requirement that boring work in rotary & percussive motion to achieve.

圖 462　鑽堡機鑽孔作業依照地質狀況加裝套管的態樣

Figure 462. Casing was used on the suitability of the ground condition during the drilling operation.

圖 463　鑽堡機鑽孔作業暫停進行鑽桿加長的態樣

Figure 463. Scene of the drilling machine that suspended for the drill rod to has been lengthened which was inserted into the casing.

圖 464　現場鑽孔作業達到設計的深度，將停機依序拆卸鑽桿。

Figure 464. When the drilling work which required depth has been achieved then the work of follow up must be prepared that drilling rod were extracted by rotating out via the drilling machine.

圖 465　鑽孔達到預定深度即進行灌漿作業

Figure 465. The cement grout has been prepared in the mixer tank, when fixed depth on charge length was achieved.

圖 466　水泥漿經由塑膠管高壓灌注，將鑽孔全部灌滿。

Figure 466. The cement grout was injected with high pressure with plastic grouting pipe until the drilled hole is full.

圖 467　作業人員將鋼鍵從預留套管慢慢推進滑入的態樣

Figure 467. Scene of workers grasped a piece of strand tendon that they were to inserted into the casing slowly.

圖 468　鋼鍵尾端則使用鑽堡機螺旋座頂住，將鋼鍵推進預定的深度。

Figure 468. Worker operated thehead of rotating axial to push the the tendons to reached the required depth as fixed length of ground anchor.

圖 469　當水泥漿溢出管口後，套管陸續被鑽堡機拉出進行拆卸。

Figure 469. When net grout flows out from the top of drilled hole that drilling casing was extracted by rotating out via the drilling machine.

圖 470　地錨的鋼鍵被錨碇後，其預留的鋼鍵外露的態樣。

Figure 470. The retained strand tendon was exposed outside of the king piles with lagging after tendon was finished in bonding.

圖 471　電焊工正進行地錨安裝於水平圍令支撐座架的焊接固定，以利地錨安裝。

Figure 471. Typical dead men of anchor brackets were welded on the king pile which support the wales & favorable the installation of anchor head.

圖 472　擋土壁之開挖面進行安裝第一段橫擋的態樣

Figure 472. Two ranks of wales in first stage which had been placed on the typical dead men of anchor brackets.

圖 473　現場進行安裝第二段橫擋的態樣

Figure 473. Scene of wales was hoisting & installation in second stage at site.

圖 474　油壓千斤頂應附有經校正之壓力表，以隨時均可讀出鋼鍵所受之拉力。

Figure 474. Calibrational pressure gauge with hydraulic jack that Reading of prestressing force to strand tendon was check in any time.

圖 475　作業主管檢視地錨錨頭施加預力的千斤頂有無異狀發生

Figure 475. Supervisor inspected the tendons & jack which endured the pre-stress enforce that was any abnormal condition occurred in progressing.

圖 476　現場施加預力的讀數回饋至轉換公式的參數，以確認預力施工有無達到地錨設計的標準。

Figure 476. Data of reading with pressure gauge was operated to the transfer formula for the data is certificated to meet the standard of ground anchor design.

圖 477　施加預力構件說明：1. 台座；2. 承壓鈑；3. 千斤頂；4. 握線夾頭；5. 楔子夾片；6. 鋼鍵

Figure 477. Components of pre-stress enforced as 1. pedestal 2. bearing plate 3. hydraulic jack 4. tendon holderbat 5. wedge 6. tendons.

圖 478　錨頭完成預力施加後，即將鋼鍵預留 20CM 其餘剪除。

Figure 478. The strand tendons were retained in 20 centimeters length after anchor which was completed pre-stress to strand tendons.

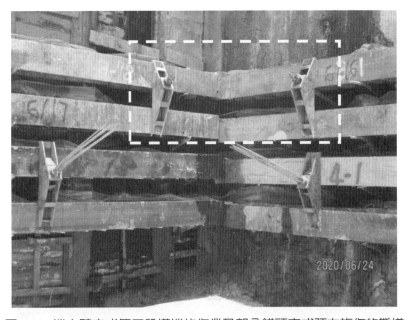

圖 479　擋土壁完成第二段橫擋的作業及部分錨頭完成預力施作的態樣

Figure 479. When the wales have been finished in 2nd stage on the retaining wall & some of anchorage tendons were accomplished the pre-stress work which appearance on the anchor head.

3. 檔土壁支撐作業安全衛生管理的要點 The strut work of retaining wall that the crucial skill of safety & health management.

圖 480　H 型鋼材料吊掛作業必採對向 2 點吊掛，以防止飛落意外。

Figure 480. To prevent the falling accident occurred that H type steel should be hoisted in two points at different side for balance.

圖 481　地錨的鋼鍵製作區必須圈圍有臨時性的安全防護

Figure 481. The strand tendons were fabricated at site where should have temporary safety guard installation around the zone.

圖 482　鑽堡機進行地錨鑽孔作業時，作業主管必須在場監督管理。

Figure 482. Supervisor should take observation & engagement at work place when drilling work was in progressing.

6-4 地上結構分項工程安全衛生規劃暨執行要點 Essential work planning & executed of safety & health for the sectoral work of superstructures.

圖 483　住者有其屋的政策呈現出城市之美的寫照

Figure 483. Image of city beautiful which was appeared by means of the policies that residents shall have own's house.

一、營建工藝的基本原理 The basic principle of construction workermanship.

點、線、面的意涵 Implication of spot, line, plane.

「點」代表一個空間裡的一個位置，沒有長度、沒有高度、沒有方向，純粹存在於零次元的非物質存在。世間萬物都會巧妙運用到的點、線、面的原理，在學設計的基礎中，是一塊重要根基，也就是說，學設計都必須要需要學到點線面構圖原理。地球、太陽、月亮三位一體在宇宙瀚海中也是點的代表，因爲人們在仰望觀看天際時，因位置不同和角度不同，就會有不同的感覺及看法。

「線」的存在意義是長度，是一個點到另一個點移動軌跡造成的長度。線比點還來得有發揮性，因爲線有長度、寬度、形狀概念，甚至還能變化出曲線、幾何線、不規則線等各種線性造形。

「面」的元素通常都是由點與線結合出一個範圍，產生出另一種元素，也就是說，面就是點跟線的延伸。面一定是有位置、形狀和面積，因爲都是延伸過來的，所以面的最大特色在於不管用什麼方式，只要用線跟點去結合，通常會變化出更多形狀。三角形擁有指標性、方向感，均衡出複雜感受及神奇的概念，

「體」是什麼？意思是一個立體，當不同的面於不同的方向，並在邊緣的位置連在一起，便形成體。體是有長度、闊度及高度，它規模著立體的空間和位置。

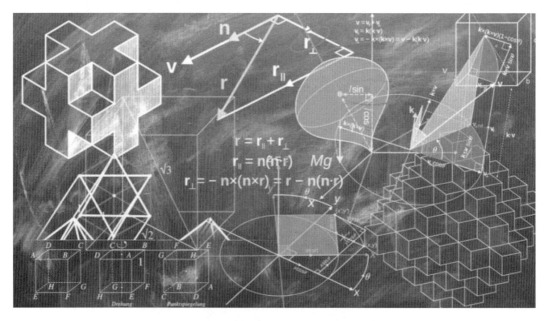

圖 484　圖學呈現點、線、面、體的概念

Figure 484. Conception of spot, line, plane, solidity which were shown on the graphic.

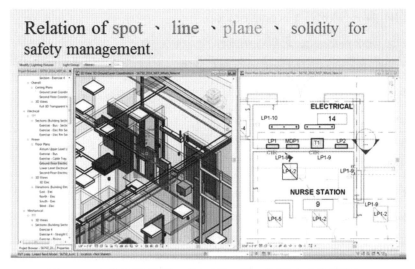

圖 485 工作屬性有點、線、面、體，均與安全有關係。

Figure 485. Work attribute of spot, line, plane, solidity with the relationship of safety.

二、營建工程安全衛生管理的精義 Detailed exposition of safety & health management which was for the construction project.

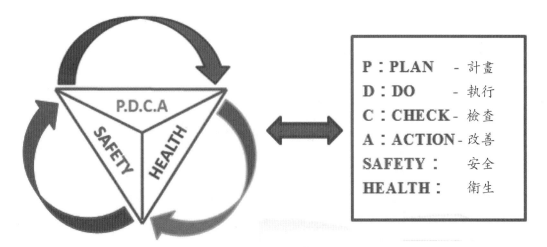

P：PLAN	－ 計畫
D：DO	－ 執行
C：CHECK	－ 檢查
A：ACTION	－ 改善
SAFETY：	安全
HEALTH：	衛生

圖 486 工程安全衛生管理鑽石定律

Figure 486. Diamond law was for the safety & health management of construction.

(一) 安全的內涵，SAFETY's connotation.

1. S：Study the work procedure. 研析作業流程

2. A：Analyze the the potential hazard. 分析潛在危害

3. F：Find the strategy to resolve. 擬定解決對策

4. E：Eliminate the risk of method. 消除作業風險

5. T：Training in constantly. 教育訓練不中斷

6. Y：Year by year in your mind. 永遠銘記在心

(二) 衛生的內涵，HEALTH's connotation.

1. H：Head should wear the hard hat. 頭必戴安全帽

2. E：Eye should wear the goggle. 眼睛戴護目鏡

3. A：Arm should wear the protective sleeves. 手臂要穿戴防護套

4. L：Leg wears the protective equipment. 腳穿戴防護具

5. T：Toe wears the safety boots. 腳趾穿戴安全鞋

6. H：Hand wears the gloves. 雙手穿戴手套

(三) P, D, C, A 管理機制的內涵

　　Connotation of management mechanim was plan, do, check, action.

1. P：Plan in comprehensive. 規劃階段必須全面考量

2. D：Do must be certainly. 執行階段必須確實

3. C：Check in cautious. 查核階段必須謹慎

4. A：Action shall be carefully. 改善階段必須小心

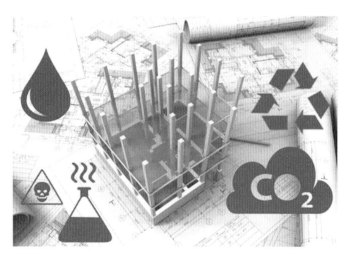

圖 487　工程全方位優質安全衛生管理

Figure 487. Safety & health were in premium management of omni bearing.

三、導入 BIM 技術研討作業風險及減災對策 Leading in the BIM to the risk of work & strategy of reduce the disaster.

(一) 運用建築資訊模型 BIM（Building Information Modeling）來強化作業安全衛生管理 Operated the BIM to enforce the safety & health management

近年來營建業掀起一股熱潮，導入建築資訊模型（Building Information Modeling, BIM），此技術應用於營建工程的生命週期，具有極佳優勢。BIM 技術可以有效整合各階段不同工項的圖面資訊，並利用 3D 視覺化檢討提升溝通協調的優勢，預先發現並解決問題，達到優質化設計的目的，進而提升整體工程品質，期望能夠在施工期間達標零職災的政策。

(二) 應用 BIM 技術導入工程管理的優勢如下說明 BIM was applied the technique to leading into the construction management that was superior as follow description.

1. 透過 BIM 模型以三度空間整合及溝通各專業間之介面關係。
2. 分項工程作業前應用 BIM 的導入，可於作業前了解危害辨識及風險評估作業，研討出對策，減少職業災害的發生。
3. 產出各作業系統的碰撞報告於施工前期預先得知，以利擬定完善的施工計畫。
4. 配合工程進度，建立 4D 之工程進度模擬，檢討施工可行性，施工前準備及調整重疊施工，以減少風險的發生。
5. 材料數量予以量化及估計資源量，避免未來不必要的浪費。

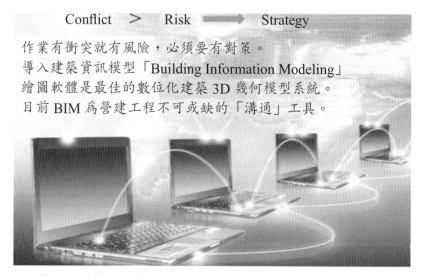

圖 488　建築資訊模型是當今可視性影像達成溝通的最佳工具

Figure 488. BIM was the best visible image & communicate instrument in nowadays.

圖 489　作業前將 BIM 導入解決共同作業的衝突點，節省時間及成本並減災。

Figure 489. To resolved the conflicted point to save the time, direct cost & reduced disaster that was leading in the BIM prior the work in operation.

6-5 建築鋼筋混凝土結構工程 Structure construction of architecture was reinforced concrete

買新屋的消費者會問？RC、SRC、SC 哪一種結構比較好？目前臺灣最常用於建築的三種結構分別為 RC（鋼筋混凝土）、SRC（鋼骨鋼筋混凝土）和 SC（鋼骨樑柱外面噴塗防火披覆使用）。

一、鋼筋混凝土工程階層構築重點作業概述 Summary of reinforced concrete construction was in different proceres.

房子的建造是用鋼筋、模板及混凝土興建成三位一體，稱為鋼筋混凝土結構，其柱體會以很多的箍筋、繫筋，緊密圍束柱的每一根大號主筋，且大樑每一根大號主筋也會有樑箍筋緊密連結以確保安全。鋼筋混凝土屬較剛硬的結構，地震來襲時搖晃度小，舒適性、防水性、隔音性也較佳，臺灣九成房子都是用鋼筋混凝土興建，是最傳統、也是業界技術最純熟的建築工法。

圖 490　開挖面整平後，基礎大底澆置混凝土，俟乾涸後進行放樣。

Figure 490. Laying off was progressing after placing one layer of concrete until in final set after the earth of foundation has been graded.

圖 491　筏基底版進行鋼筋配置及紮結的態樣

Figure 491. Scene of rebar has been placed & wire tied work on the bottom layer of slab in raft foundation.

圖 492　筏基底版鋼筋配置及中間柱周邊鋼筋加勁紮結的態樣

Figure 492. Reinforced rebars were fix with wire tired around the center post on the bottom layer slab of raft foundation.

圖 493　筏基四周地樑進行鋼筋組立紮結的態樣

Figure 493. Scene of girder which rebars was erected & wire tired in exterior portion of raft foundation.

圖 494　筏基與地樑進行鋼筋組立紮結的態樣

Figure 494. Scene of girders in raft foundation where rebar was erected & wire tired in the crossover.

圖 495　筏基坑地樑進行模板組立

Figure 495. Wooden form work of girders which has been assembled to the raft foundation.

圖 496　地樑澆置完成用帆布包覆，進行部分基坑回填土的作業。

Figure 496. Girder was wrapped with canvas after pouring the concrete that backhoe material was dumped to the pits of foundation.

圖 497　基坑回填土作業前，先行完成保護地樑品質的包覆作業。

Figure 497. Protection of girders with canvases to keep the quality in required prior the dump soil to backfill the pits of foundation.

圖 498　地下室樓地板於混凝土澆置前，均做好安全及品質的防護。

Figure 498. All safety & quality control have been done on the slab of basement that was prior the pouring concrete in operation.

圖 499　地下結構樓地板進行混凝土澆置的態樣

Figure 499. Scene of pouring concrete was in progressing on the slab of substructure

圖 500　地下結構分間牆進行模板組立及鋼筋紮結作業態樣

Figure 500. There was the form works of compartment's wall & rebar erected which was in progressing at substructure.

圖 501　施工架組立完整，以利地下結構進行柱鋼筋紮結作業。

Figure 501. Scaffold should assembly completely meet the regulation for the rebar erected work of column of substructure.

圖 502　完整的施工作業平台以利地下結構外牆進行模板作業的態樣

Figure 502. Working platform has been manufactured fot the board sheathing of exterior wall of substructure.

圖 503　地下結構外牆混凝土澆置完成後，即進行擋土牆 H 型鋼樁拔出作業的態樣。

Figure 503. H type steel pile was extracted with vibratory hydraulic driver when the exterior wall which complication of pouring concrete at site.

圖 504　地上結構柱鋼筋進行組立紮結之前，先行組裝完整的施工架作業平台之態樣。

Figure 504. The work platform should be assemblied completely before the rebar erected work to column of superstructure.

圖 505　施工架作業平台應有上下設備及要求鋼筋工使用安全帶

Figure 505. Work platform which has one stairs mounted on the scaffold & ask the rebar workers should wear the harness on the scaffold.

圖 506　柱鋼筋組立紮結完成後，水電線盒安裝及模板組模立即進場作業的態樣。

Figure 506. Rebar work has been finished of colummn that there were workers of formwork & plumbers to access for working at site.

圖 507　柱模板組立及斜撐加勁後，則進行樑的底模板支撐組立的作業。

Figure 507. Beam soffit was installed & struted with adjustable steel props after boarding of column has been finished with raked adjustable steel prop.

圖 508　分間牆模板組立完成，模板工檢查螺桿並且加固作業的態樣。

Figure 508. Workers check the sheathing of wall that who screwed to enforce the iron screw ties on the verticle steel stud for safety.

圖 509　模板工進行樑模底板使用單鋼管支撐作業的態樣

Figure 509. Beam plywood soffits were propped with the adjustable steel props by form workers.

圖 510 樑模底板使用單鋼管支撐完成組立作業的態樣

Figure 510. Scene of the beam plywood soffits were propped with the adjustable steel props in crossover at site.

圖 511 樓板部分的樑模板組立完成作業的態樣

Figure 511. Scene of beam construction has been completed which is parts of slab construction.

圖 512　樓板的版模貫材及格柵完成與樑側模相互釘結組立完成作業的態樣

Figure 512. Joists stacked on the ledgers was parts of slab prop frame which was fixed to the edge beam formwork sides with nails.

圖 513　依照施工圖的要求樓板襯板及樑模相互釘結完成作業的態樣

Figure 513. According the working drawing that plastic sheathing & beam side shuttering has been fixed completely of slab construction.

圖 514　當責工程師檢查樓板高程及樑間距尺寸完成後，版及樑的鋼筋進場吊放完成作業的
　　　　態樣。

Figure 514. Rebars for using of beam & slab which hoister was delieveried on the slab after duty's
engineer has checked the sizes & elevation of beam & others.

圖 515　挑高樓板的模板作業採用框式施工架是最安全的作法

Figure 515. Formworks of high elevated slab construction that frame scaffolding has been used at site
which the best facility for safety.

圖 516　框式鋼管式施工架進行組立作業時，於適當高度設置防墜安全網。

Figure 516. Spread & tied the safety nets which was beneath the scaffolding to prevented fall accident during the assembly work in progressing.

圖 517　框式鋼管式施工架必須於適當的地點設置人員上下設備

Figure 517. Stair access of scaffolding was required to assembly for using at the proper location.

圖 518　框式鋼管式施工架上層鋪設模板作為後續施工的作業平台

Figure 518. Wooden form as lower sleeper was placed on the top of frame scaffolding as working platform for the follow-up work.

圖 519　挑高樓板的作業平台符合安全規定，以利後續樑版模板作業。

Figure 519. Working platform should meet the safety regulation which on the high elevated scaffolding to benefit the beam construction.

圖 520　鋼筋工進場進行樑鋼筋搬運組立及紮結作業的態樣

Figure 520. Scene of rebar workers were deliveried & erected the rebar of beam on the slab construction.

圖 521　樓板底層鋼筋完成後，水電工進行配管安裝作業的態樣。

Figure 521. Plumber has the installation work of boxes & PVC pipes on the slab where lower layer of rebar has been done.

圖 522　鋼筋工進行樓梯版鋼筋配置及紮結作業的態樣

Figure 522. Scene of rebar work at stairway between stories that worker has arranged the rebar to fix with tie wires.

圖 523　樓板鋼筋配置紮結期間，特別設置簡易式尿桶供作業人員方便使用的態樣。

Figure 523. There was one set of convenient urinal put up at proper location of slab which available to workers.

圖 524　樓板配筋勘驗完成，進行混凝土澆置的態樣。

Figure 524. Scene of pouring concrete was in progressing on the slab after the rebar arrangement which
was inspected by professional engineer.

圖 525　室內磚砌隔間的紅磚材料配送作業已完成的態樣

Figure 525. Material of brick was delievered with worker in the interior room that was used for the
partitional brick wall work.

圖 526　室內隔間紅磚實心牆完成及門楣設置固定的態樣

Figure 526. Scene of solid brick wall has been completed that lintel was laid onto of the door space of indoor compartments.

圖 527　室內紅磚隔間牆完成後，進行泥作粉刷材料進場的態樣。

Figure 527. Brick finishing mortar as cement & sand was delivered with worker after solid brick wall of compartment has been completed.

圖 528　泥作粉刷作業需備妥安全作業平台及上下設備的態樣

Figure 528. Ladder mounted on the working platform with guardrail should been prepared for the using of cement masons.

圖 529　樓底版披土作業需有安全的作業平台及使用勾掛安全帶作業的態樣

Figure 529. Workers wore the safety belt & used the big hook on the guardrail at mobile platform to laid adhesive mortar under ceiling in progressing.

圖 530　行人步道景觀進行植栽綠化作業的態樣

Figure 530. Scene of raise of trees & plants was working in the recreational area of pedestrians' path.

二、混凝土構築作業階段安衛管理要項（作業人員的部分）The crucial skill of Safety & health management was executed in project of concrete framed work. (Part of access worker).

圖 531　工地警衛室對進場作業人員嚴格核對做好安全的態樣

Figure 531. Security guard of work site took the strictly observed to the access worker.

圖532　工地設置人臉辨識器，落實進場人員管制作業的態樣。

Figure 532. Installed the facial recognition system which was to controlled the access workers' identification into the work site.

圖533　工地設置閉路電視監視重要地點，防止任何意外發生的態樣。

Figure 533. To prevented the accident happened at work site that closed circuit television was installed the major spots for observation.

圖 534　工務所就分項作業前的危害辨識進行與承商溝通的態樣

Figure 534. Held the communication meeting to variant contractor that was studied the hazard identification in together prior the work in progressing at site.

圖 535　工地主管簡報施工期間安全衛生執行作業的態樣

Figure 535. Supervisor was invited to report the executive management of safety & health during the construction period at headquarters.

圖 536　每日針對工地的巡檢缺失召開會議進行改善的態樣

Figure 536. Meeting of Safety deficiencies was hold to subcontractors that deficiencies was illustrated & improved in timelimited when site inspection in daily.

圖 537　察覺工地發生嚴重缺失時，除立即停工外，並現場解說要求立即將缺失改善的態樣。

Figure 537. Serious safety deficiencies wer inspected at work place that safety supervisor gave the suspended order & express the dangerious result which deficiencies should be improved immediately.

圖 538 工務所定期舉行實兵演練，如侷限空間作業救援的態樣。

Figure 538. Actual drill was held on the regular time at work site that was rescued operation of confine space.

圖 539 依規定使用電梯井進行吊掛作業需穿戴背負式安全帶的態樣

Figure 539. Worker wore the full body harness with big snap hook & tied to the O-ring on the wall to move the material as hoisting operation from the lift shaft.

圖 540　模板工依規定配戴安全護目鏡作業的態樣

Figure 540. Worker was required to wear the safety glasses during the form work at work place.

三、混凝土構築作業階段安衛管理要項（設備的部分）The crucial skill of Safety & health management was executed in project of concrete framed work.(Part of facilities).

圖 541　手工具的漏電檢測採月份色標管理作業的態樣

Figure 541. Tag of color code in month was used in the hand tool for leak testing.

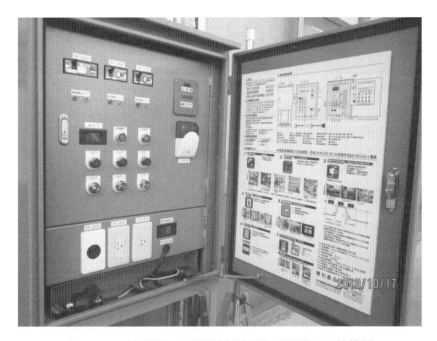

圖 542　工地設置一台漏電檢測器檢測電動工具的態樣

Figure 542. There was one set of leak detector for the hand tools to prepare at work site.

圖 543　手工具漏電檢測合格及貼上當月色標作為識別的態樣

Figure 543. There were hand tools which past the leak detector test then qualified safety color tag of that month was post on it.

圖 544　地下結構筏基作業時，必須於適當位置設置上下設備的態樣。

Figure 544. Access step ladder was put up at proper location when raft foundation work was in progressing.

圖 545　施工構台的安全走道規劃及安全護欄的態樣

Figure 545. Safety path was painted as yellow color on the platform with guardrail of strut working area.

圖 546　依法令規定施工構台的覆工鈑需張掛安全防墜網的態樣

Figure 546. Safety net was spread & tied tighten below the decks of platform which comply with the act.

圖 547　樓板進行混凝土作業期間，樓梯要設置臨時的防墜設施。

Figure 547. Temporary guardrail of fall prevent facilities was installed at stair way between stories during the construction work in progressing.

圖 548　電梯井進行模板組立階段需有臨時性防墜設施的態樣

Figure 548. Temporary fall prevent facilities as closed down with wooden form at lift shaft.

圖 549　電梯井進行牆模板組立時，其作業平台下方應張掛安全防墜網。

Figure 549. Safety net should be spread beneath the platform during the boarding of lift shaft which was
installed with worker.

圖 550　模板作業的桌面圓盤鋸需安裝鋸齒接觸預防裝置，防止切傷意外發生。

Figure 550. Table circular saw should have mounted the saw guard to prevented the cutting accident be occurred at work place.

圖 551　鋼筋切斷機的按鈕開關必須有防水設施的態樣

Figure 551. The button of switch box that function was for waterproof to rebar cutting machine at site.

圖 552　地面預留孔需設置安全護欄及明顯警告標示的態樣

Figure 552. Retain hatch of the slab where should have the guard rail with apparent warning sign.

圖 553　垃圾輸送管道設置於室內樓板預留孔的態樣

Figure 553. Rubbish chutes was mounted on the retain shaft between the stories.

圖 554　電梯井的防墜柵欄及背負式安全帶勾掛使用鋼索的態樣

Figure 554. Steel wire rope was mounted on the ceiling with one lanyard for the using to worker who has the hoisting operation at lift shaft that worker should wear the full body harness.

圖 555　電梯井內設置安全防墜網的態樣

Figure 555. Safety nets were spread & tied tight which mounted the inner of lift shaft in each stories.

圖 556　樓層管道間預留孔設置安全護欄及防墜網的態樣

Figure 556. Retain hatch of pipeline where should installed the guardail with safety net.

圖 557　電梯井防墜設施設置安全柵欄及張掛警告標示的態樣

Figure 557. Safety grids were installed at lift shaft with apparentwarning sigh of piece canvas.

圖 558　各樓層均設置臨時供水和洗滌用沉砂桶的態樣

Figure 558. Sediment bucket & temporary water supply were prepared & install at each floor by site office.

圖 559　結構體施工期間已完成的室內樓梯必須設置安全欄杆的態樣

Figure 559. Guard rails were erected on the stairway of each floor after concrete construction has been completelied.

圖 560 室內樓梯於泥作粉刷期間採用防墜網吊垂方式的態樣

Figure 560. Durring the mason construction of indoor that safety net was spread & tied from the upper floor to the lower floor to prevented fall accident occurred.

圖 561 施工架材料進場需要求承商檢附法令規定的材質證明

Figure 561. Subcontractor should submit the material certificate of scaffold which was improved the quality comply with the act's requirement.

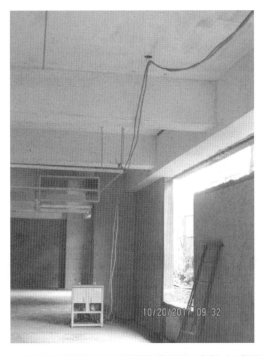

圖 562　室內的臨時用電電纜線均需架高防止感電意外

Figure 562. Cable line of temporary power supply was elevate on the wall that was to prevent the shock accident at work site.

圖 563　室內結構體的修繕均需搭設施工架防止意外發生的態樣

Figure 563. Repair work of structial construction was prepared the scaffold for the fix work of indoor.

圖 564　搭設移動式施工架以利室內結構體的分項作業執行

Figure 564. Mobile scaffold was erected for the variant work which was executed of indoor.

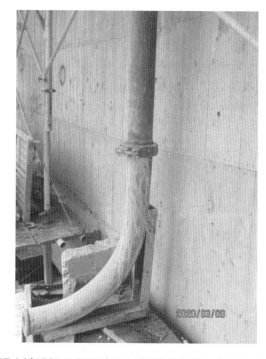

圖 565　混凝土輸送管必須固定於結構體的外側，以防倒塌意外發生。

Figure 565. For the safety to prevent the collapse incident happened concrete pumping pipeline should mount firmly on the structure wall.

圖 566　室外施工架除定期安全檢查之外，並且保持止滑踏板的清潔。

Figure 566. Scaffold erected completely for using that was inspected in regular time for safety include the working platform where must be tidy.

圖 567　施工架的上下設備，其防塵網採用不同顏色以示區別的態樣。

Figure 567. Stair tower of scaffold which around was wrapped with gray nets that was much different overed.

圖 568　施工架的防塵網於中央氣象局發布颱風來襲前應完成綑綁準備，防止施工架因風壓因素造成倒塌意外發生。

Figure 568. Scaffold safety net should be bound completely with rope in safety to prevent the incident happen which caused by the wind pressure that work has been done before land storm warning which announced with central weather bureau.

四、混凝土構築作業階段安衛管理要項（精進的部分）The crucial skill of Safety & health management was executed in project of concrete framed work.(Part of refine).

圖 569　樑模板採地面組裝態樣

Figure 569. Scene of beam formwork was made on the ground.

圖 570 樑模底板及側板採地面組裝完成的態樣

Figure 570. Beam formwork as beam bottom plywood has fixed to the runners with both sides shuttering that has assemblied completely on the ground.

圖 571 樑模板採地面組裝是降低人員墜落高風險的最佳對策之一

Figure 571. There was one of best strategy to reduce the risk of fall accident that beam formwork has assembly on the ground.

圖 572　樑模板採吊掛裝置的態樣

Figure 572. Beam formwork has been fixed completely as load was lifting to the proper elevation for connecting the column with mobile crane.

圖 573　鋼筋加工材料進場不得使用鋼筋作為吊架進行吊掛作業

Figure 573. All processing material of rebar which was delievried & lifting operation at site that sling was made of rebar which was not approved.

圖 574　鋼筋加工材料進場必須使用合格吊籃及額定荷重的標誌

Figure 574. Processing material of rebar as hanger which was lifted at work site should use the cage with the warning sign of rated load.

圖 575　混凝土結構施工期間因下大雨造成室內樓梯間大水傾瀉的態樣

Figure 575. Sight of rainfall was pour down from the stair due to the gap or open space of structure when the raining day of concrete construction in progressing.

圖576　混凝土結構施工期間防止室外雨水進入室內，其對策之一是樓板預留孔要完全封閉。

Figure 576. There was one manner of strategy to prevent the rainfall from outsite to inside that was sealed the gap & open spaces at slab during the concrete construction in progressing.

圖 577　施工期間防止室外雨水由樓梯間進入室內，其對策之二是室內樓梯旁跳層設置導水槽。

Figure 577. Conduct chutes of water were mounted on stringer of indoor stairway which was the second manner to prevent the water came from the stair space of top floor.

圖 578　室內樓梯旁設置導水槽，於底部集水盤外接水管，將雨水排放到室外。

Figure 578. The basin of conduct chute which bottom connect one drainage pipe to discharged water
　　　　　from the outdoor.

6-6 鋼骨鋼筋混凝土結構工程 Structure construction was steel reinforced concrete

　　SRC 結構則是結合「鋼筋混凝土」和「鋼骨」的結構方式，樑柱中間以鋼骨支撐，外圍再用十五至二十公分的混凝土包覆，混凝土中亦會有大號主鋼筋及箍筋，由鋼筋及鋼骨共同作用，讓建築有較強的韌性以及抗拉能力。SRC 比 RC 多了內部鋼骨的配置，有較強的韌性與抗拉能力，在樓層較高的建案中，與 RC 設計相較，可略微縮小柱的斷面尺寸，故在高層建築中會以 SRC 結構設計為主，主要是為減少柱所占的空間面積及縮短施工作業的時間等，本節逐介紹鋼結構採用地下逆打工法及地上順打工法的施工流程。

圖 579　逆打工法及順打工法鋼骨鋼筋混凝土結構施工中的態樣

Figure 579. Steel reinforced concrete as SRC which construction was used top down method for substructure & bottom up method for superstructure.

一、鋼骨鋼筋混凝土工程階層構築作業概述：上部結構工程──順打工法 Steel reinforced concrete construction which summary was in different procedures: Superstructure construction adapted for bottom-up method.

圖 580　基樁鋼筋籠組裝完成後，工程師進行檢查是否合乎規定。

Figure 580. Engineers checked the fabricated reinforcement cage of pile which should meet the requirement of working drawing.

圖 581　逆打鋼柱進場放置作業現場的態樣

Figure 581. Plunge column was placed at site after accessing.

圖 582　逆打鋼柱進行吊放的態樣

Figure 582. Plunge column was lifting in progressing at site.

圖 583　逆打鋼柱吊放於基樁內並安放在鋼樑托架上的態樣

Figure 583. Plunge column of top down method was placed onto the beams as bracket which has been lifting into the casing.

圖 584　逆打鋼柱上部接合一根托柱，以利定位及定心作業的態樣。

Figure 584. There was a piece of H shape column which fixed plunge column with bolts for the next work of fixed location & elevation.

圖 585 逆打鋼柱高程及定位確定後，則進行混凝土澆置的態樣。

Figure 585. Pouring concrete into the pile bored was ready after the plunge column which was in fixed location & elevation.

圖 586 第一層開挖後，逆打鋼柱顯露的態樣。

Figure 586. Plunge column was appeared after excavating in first layer.

圖 587 逆打鋼柱周邊進行反力支撐墩座混凝土作業的態樣

Figure 587. Rebar work of thrust block has been finished which around the plunge column.

圖 588 逆打鋼柱周邊鋼筋作業已完成，將繼續進行混凝土作業的態樣。

Figure 588. Scope of plunge column where is going to finish the concete work even the rebar work has done.

圖 589　液壓千斤頂安裝於逆打鋼柱與反力支撐墩座間將進行鋼柱校正作業的態樣

Figure 589. Scene of the calibration of plunge column that hydraulic jack was mounted between the plunge column & the thrust block.

圖 590　現場液壓千斤頂進行逆打鋼柱校正作業的態樣

Figure 590. Scene of the calibration of plunge column that hydraulic jack was operated in progressing at site.

圖 591　上部結構的鋼柱進場準備下料的態樣

Figure 591. Steel column of superstructure was delieveried & unloading at site with the link car.

圖 592　鋼構主組裝人員準備自動脫鉤器勾卦鋼柱吊耳的態樣

Figure 592. Steel installer held four sets of verticle lifting closing clamp (ratchet release shackle) to hitch the fixed lifting point.

圖 593　作業主管複檢勾卦鋼柱吊耳的自動脫鉤器是否符合安全要求

Figure 593. There was initial requirement that supervisor of steel work was to recheck the latch of vertical lifting closing clamp (ratchet release shackle) which inserted firmly or not.

圖 594　作業主管複檢吊耳的自動脫鉤器符合安全則鋼柱進行吊掛

Figure 594. Steel column was lifting in progressing after rechecking the ratchet release shackle was finished with supervisor at site.

圖 595　上部結構的鋼柱被吊放一樓作業現場的態樣

Figure 595. Steel column of superstructure was deliveried to the 1st floor slab which layed near the work place.

圖 596　第一節鋼柱已被吊放準備和逆打鋼柱相互連結的態樣

Figure 596. Steel column of 1st segment was deliveried onto the plunge column that was connected together at work place.

圖 597 鋼構組裝人員使用連結調整器,將第一節鋼柱和逆打鋼柱相互連結的態樣。

Figure 597. Scene of steel column were connected together with steel structure connection adjuster clamp as 1st segment & plunge column

圖 598 現場上構鋼柱與逆打鋼柱採用鋼構連結調整器接合固定

Figure 598. Steel column of superstructure was connected to plunge column with steel structure connection adjuster clamp at site.

圖 599　現場上構鋼樑正進行高拉力螺栓鎖固鋼柱的連接鈑的態樣

Figure 599. Flexible beam of superstructure was connected to rigid rafter of column with high tension bolts

圖 600　鋼構主樑進行吊掛就位和柱組裝作業的態樣

Figure 600. Master beam was lifting to the fixed position that was installed & connected the column.

圖 601　鋼樑於吊掛前需先安裝防墜設施，如垂直桿柱及安全母索。

Figure 601. Safety rod with life line was mounted on the top flange of steel beam as prevent fall facilities.

圖 602　工地鋼骨構架繼續進行吊掛及組裝作業的態樣

Figure 602. Frame of steel structure was installed & connected with installers at site.

圖 603　工地鋼骨構架已完成吊掛組裝及安全網完成張掛作業的態樣

Figure 603. Steel frame has been installed & connected of bolts was in completion with safety nets was stretched completely at site.

圖 604　現場工程師進行第一節鋼構柱樑吊掛組裝，完成部分垂直度的校正。

Figure 604. Site engineer used the transit surveying to has calibration of steel column that 1st segment of steel structure frame has been installed completely at site.

圖 605　固定式起重機進行鋼柱吊掛作業的態樣

Figure 605. Scene of steel column was in lifting operation with tower cranes at site.

圖 606　鋼構測量校正作業完成後，進行焊接固定作業。

Figure 606. Welding work was in progressing with welder after steel structure frame has been calibrated already at site.

圖 607　鋼構電焊人員因作業方便需要採用安全吊籃式作業平台

Figure 607. Welder used the platform of basket to do the welding work that it was safety & convenient.

圖 608　電焊人員正熔切鋼柱上混凝土壓送管的續接套頭

Figure 608. Welder used the Oxy Acetylene cutting torch to cut the coupler of concrete filled in tube of steel column.

圖 609　鋼柱內灌漿完成數日後，進行灌漿孔封鈑作業的態樣。

Figure 609. The steel plate was meld to seal the hole on the steel column after concrete filled in tube has been finished in few days after.

圖 610　現場鋼筋工進行鋼柱包覆型鋼筋組配紮結的作業

Figure 610. Rebar worker was in progressing to erect the rebar in cladding shape for steel column of 1st segament.

圖 611 鋼柱的包覆型配筋與連接樑鋼筋紮結完成的態樣

Figure 611. Steel column was erected with rebar in cladding shape which scene was showed the completed of beam & column animation.

圖 612 鋼柱與連接樑進行側邊模板組立的態樣

Figure 612. Steel column connected linked beam which was installed shuttering work in progressing at site.

圖 613　鋼構柱及樑的鋼筋與連續壁周邊樑的配筋已完成的態樣

Figure 613. Scene of completion which was the rebar method of steel framework as 1st segment with surrounding connected beams of diaphragm wall.

圖 614　一樓鋼結構樑的包覆型鋼筋紮結完成的態樣

Figure 614. Rebar work as cladding method of beams in 1st slab has been completed at work place.

圖 615　一樓板的鋼骨構架包覆型鋼筋與連續壁周邊樑相互組配的態樣

Figure 615. Ther was an animation of rebar work as cladding method to steel frame in 1st slab which combined the surrounding connected beam of diaphragm wall.

圖 616　工期的考量施工中，也有遮斷層的規劃。

Figure 616. There was obstructed layer of deck installation on the proper story according to the plan which was great benefit to the progress of construction duration.

圖 617　鋼筋工進行鋼樑包覆型鋼筋組立紮結作業的態樣

Figure 617. There was two rebar worker that has the cladding method to the beam in progressing at work place.

圖 618　水電工進行鋼樑預留孔管線安裝作業的態樣

Figure 618. Scene of plumber inserted the pipes into the reserved holes of the beam at site.

圖 619　鋼樑包覆型鋼筋組立紮結與牆筋連結完成作業的態樣

Figure 619. There was the animation of rebar work as cladding method to the beam which connected the rebar of the wall.

圖 620　模板工進行鋼柱及牆模板組立現場作業的態樣

Figure 620. Scene of wooden form work was in progressing that shuttering of column & sheathing of wall were installed at workplace.

圖 621　鋼柱的模板組立現場已完工作業的態樣

Figure 621. Scene of shuttering of column has been installed completely at site.

圖 622　隔間牆的模板組立現場進行作業的態樣

Figure 622. Scene of sheathing of compartment wall has been installing in progressing at site.

圖 623　鋼樑包覆型鋼筋組立紮結完成則進行樑底板支撐組立作業的態樣

Figure 623. Rebar work of beam was in cladding method which wooden battens installation was propped with the adjustable steel props at site.

圖 624　樓層採用單鋼管支撐樓板模板組裝釘結作業的態樣

Figure 624. Installation wood formwork for concrete slab with propped of adjustable steel props which were beneath the slab.

圖 625　樓板模板與樑側模釘結組裝作業的態樣

Figure 625. Scene of floor sheets as plywood was fixed the side shuttering of beam with worker in progressing at site.

圖 626　樓板下層鋼筋紮結完成後，水電工則進場組裝配管作業的態樣。

Figure 626. Scene of lower rebar of slab where has been fixing completely that plumbers who accessed to had assembled the pipe line work in progressing.

圖 627　樓板上層鋼筋紮結完成後，技師們進行現場鋼筋查驗作業。

Figure 627. Registed engineer has been executing the surveillance inspection at site to the rebar work after the upper layer rebar has finished at slab of floor.

圖 628　樓板進行混凝土澆置前，座騎式及電動式整體粉光機均備妥。

Figure 628. The ride on power trowel machine & manual power trowel were prepared on the floor slab prior the pouring concrete in action.

圖 629　進場的混凝土預拌車依序瀉料作業的態樣

Figure 629. The concrete mixer trucks that were in dumping the concrete for the floor slab in sequence at work site.

圖 630　樓板澆置的混凝土其緻密度需用電動振盪整平器來作業

Figure 630. Concrete was placing on the floor slab that concrete shall be in density degree with the machine of electric roller screed.

圖 631　樓板的混凝土進行整體粉光的作業態樣

Figure 631. There was finishing concrete with power trowel smooth on the floor slab.

圖 632　樓板的混凝土進行座騎式及電動式整體粉光共同作業的態樣

Figure 632. There were one of ride on power trowel machine & power trowel smooth machine that are co-working on the floor slab.

圖 633　鋼骨結構的樓層室內泥作粉刷已準備就緒中的態樣

Figure 633. There was material of mason's work which was prepared & readiness for the indoor cement mason.

圖 634　鋼骨結構的樓層，其室內隔間大部分均採輕隔間作法。

Figure 634. Light steel frame was used in available popular of steel structure construction to indoor compartment.

圖 635　輕隔間其水電管路配置均於輕隔間夾層中的態樣

Figure 635. There were electric pipe lines which were aligned the proper location between the both sides of wall sheathing as indoor compartment.

圖 636　輕隔間內部均採岩棉填充，達到防火及隔音效果。

Figure 636. Mineral wool would be stuffed into the space of light steel frame wall to achieve the purpose of fire fighting & sound insulation.

圖 637　輕隔間封板後需先完成接縫批補後，再全面進行油漆作業。

Figure 637. The small crack of wall sheathing that was flatted with plaster after that painting work is to all scope.

一、鋼骨鋼筋混凝土工程階層構築作業概述：下部結構工程──逆打工法 Steel reinforced concrete costruction which summarry was in different procedures: Substructures Construction adapted for bottom-up method

圖 638　施工前的廠商會議以工法、安全、風險為討論重點

Figure 638. Meeting of prior the construction for subcontractors that major topic was method、safety & risk as key discussion.

圖 639　一樓板樑養護完成進行版底現場物料搬運，以利後續開挖作業。

Figure 639. Forklift has been moved the material from the plain concrete to favorable the follow up
working method after the slab of 1st which curing completely.

圖 640　破碎機具進場進行混凝土鋪面打除的態樣

Figure 640. Breaker machine accessed the work place to break the concrete of pave.

圖 641　　怪手等機具進行地下一樓土方開挖及破碎的態樣

Figure 641. Backhoe with others machine was on going to excavated & braked the soil in 1st story of basement.

圖 642　　現場伸縮手臂機具進行餘土搬運到卡車的態樣

Figure 642. Flexible hydraulic long bucket was used to delieveried the soil from the excavated area to the dump truck.

圖 643　現場工程師進行開挖面高程量測

Figure 643. Site engineers used the transit to survey the elevation of excavation in substructure.

圖 644　現場開挖完成後，進行鋼柱表面清潔的動作。

Figure 644. Worker used the tool to cleand the soil out on the column.

圖 645　現場開挖完成後，進行預留筋及牆面大肚打石的態樣。

Figure 645. Worker took the portable breaker to beat the convex concrete of wall & coated concrete of dowel after the excavation work has been completed.

圖 646　現場開挖完成後，地面鋪設兩層竹編交錯擺置，提供人員安全走動路線。

Figure 646. Concerned the workers' safety at the route of work place that two layers of bamboo knitted mat were placed on the earth after excavation work.

圖 647　現場鋪面混凝土強度提高為增強模板支撐的承載力

Figure 647. Changed to improve the strength of concrete which was enforced the supporting capacity of prop up with wooden frame work.

圖 648　現場鋪面混凝土依照放樣高程澆置完成

Figure 648. Plain concrete was placing on the earth which finished elevation of concrete should meet the mark of laying-off.

圖 649　鋪面澆置完成後，進行結構體相關位置放樣的態樣。

Figure 649. Stake man workers laying-off related size & location of structure on the pave after the pave
has placed the concrete.

圖 650　現場完成施架組裝以利鋼柱鋼筋進行組立的態樣

Figure 650. Scaffold has been erected completely for the rebar work in progressing to the steel column at
site.

圖 651　現場鋼筋工進行鋼柱主筋續接的態樣

Figure 651. Rebar worker who took major rebar to connect the coupler of steel column at site.

圖 652　現場進行鋼筋續接扭力測試的態樣

Figure 652. Major rebar of coupler connection which was in progressing of torque wrench testing.

圖 653　鋼柱鋼筋進行組立完成的態樣

Figure 653. Scene of rebar erected of cladding method was completed for steel column.

圖 654　鋼筋組立紮結完成後，進行模板組立的態樣。

Figure 654. Wood form work was in progressing at work place after rebar erected work has completion.

圖 655　現場進行逆打柱底模組立的態樣

Figure 655. Form work of column bottom mold as top-down was installed in progressing with form worker.

圖 656　周邊樑底模組立的態樣

Figure 656. Scene of beam soffit as form work was installed surrounding of wall with form workers.

圖 657　周邊樑鋼筋組立的態樣

Figure 657. Rebar work was erected & tied with workers surrounding the diaphragm wall.

圖 658　逆打樑底模組立的態樣

Figure 658. Scene of top down method that beams soffit has been installed at site.

圖 659　逆打牆底模組立的態樣

Figure 659. Scene of bottom mold as top-down wall which wood form work was installed with form workers.

圖 660　逆打牆鋼筋預埋位置放樣鑽孔的態樣

Figure 660. Bored holes on the bottom mold of wall with laying off where rebars were embedded in the top-down method.

圖 661　逆打牆預留筋綁紮的態樣

Figure 661. Scene of rebar was cast-in the wall to erected & tied in progress at site.

圖 662　樑側模組立的態樣

Figure 662. Scene of beam formwork as one side has been installed completed.

圖 663　樓板的貫材與格柵疊合組立的態樣

Figure 663. Scene of stringers & joists has been stacked together of the slab form work.

圖 664　樓板的板材組立完成的態樣

Figure 664. Scene of sheathing plywood of top-down floor slab has been completed.

圖 665　逆打工法樓板的樑鋼筋進行綁紮的態樣

Figure 665. Rebar work of beam which aligned & distributed has been progressing at floor slab as top-down method.

圖 666　樓板的版鋼筋進行綁紮的態樣

Figure 666. Rebar work of floor slab was distributed & tied in progressing at site.

圖 667　樓板版筋完成後，安置標高器的態樣。

Figure 667. The elevators were placed on the floor slab after rebar work of completion.

圖 668　混凝土伸臂式幫浦車進場整備壓送管的態樣

Figure 668. Concrete boom pump truck accessed the work site to prepare the pipeline in working.

圖 669　樓板進行混凝土澆置的態樣

Figure 669. Scene of concrete was pouring to the floor slab at site.

圖 670　樓板混凝土澆置完成後，進行溼治養護的態樣。

Figure 670. Water curing of concrete floor slab after concrete has been pouring completion.

圖 671　鋼柱包覆型鋼筋紮結完成後進行檢測的態樣

Figure 671. Surveillance inspection in the space of stirrup which rebars work of the steel column should comply with the specification.

圖 672　現場進行柱牆模尺寸確認的態樣

Figure 672. Form worker measured the accurate length of column with wall sheating in working at site.

圖 673　現場進行二次牆筋綁紮組立的態樣

Figure 673. Scene of rebar workers were in working the wall for the 2nd phase.

圖 674　現場柱牆模板組裝完成的態樣

Figure 674. Scene of form work as sheathing of wall & column has been completed at site.

圖 675　現場柱牆模板組裝完成進行混凝土澆置的態樣

Figure 675. Concrete pouring was in progressing to the column & wall with workers.

圖 676　現場柱牆混凝土澆置的高度至企口下緣，以求澆置面平整的態樣。

Figure 676. Height of pouring concrete which should met the below of rabbet chute that was a guideline for the smooth of concrete surface.

圖 677　現場柱牆拆模後上端呈現的施工縫

Figure 677. Construction joint was appeared on the top of the wall when sheating of wall has been dismantled.

圖 678　施工縫通常採用無收縮水泥灌注，並於頂部設置溢漿氣孔。

Figure 678. Construction joint where inserted one plastic tube for the mortar overflow when non-shrink mortar was grouting.

圖 679　取土口採由下逐層往上回補的樓板進行混凝土澆置的態樣

Figure 679. Rebuilded of slab as concrete work from the lower to upper floor slab where was as open space for the excavation work.

二、鋼骨鋼筋混凝土構築作業階段安衛管理要項（作業人員的部分）Safety & health management was as crucial skill of steel reinforced concrete project. (Parts of access worker).

圖 680　鋼骨鋼筋混凝土結構多採固定式起重機及施工升降機作業的態樣

Figure 680. Scene of tower crane & construction elevator were using on the steel reinforced concrete project.

圖 681　每日工具箱交談重點以作業前的危害辨識及個人防護具為要

Figure 681. There were critical points of identification of hazard prior the work & personal propective equipment to work as tool box talk in the morning.

圖 682　現場當責工程師亦穿戴背負式安全帶檢查鋼構電焊作業

Figure 682. Duty's engineers that were embraced the harness to inspected the welding work at high of steel structure at site.

圖 683　現場電焊作業人員穿戴完整的甲冑個人防護具

Figure 683. Welder wore the harness as personal protective equipment at site.

圖 684　鋼筋工於鋼樑作業中使用安全帶勾掛安全母索防止墜落意外

Figure 684. Rebar worker wore the safety belt with lifeline &snaped the big hook when he worked at height on the beam.

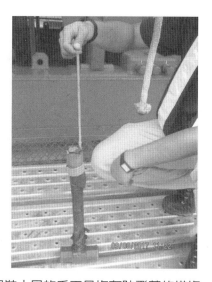

圖 685　現場鋼構組裝人員的手工具均有防飛落的措施，如鐵鎚的腕繫繩。

Figure 685. To prevent the falling accident that steel worker whose hand tool as hammer which should have the wrist sling.

三、鋼骨鋼筋混凝土構築作業階段安衛管理要項（設備的部分）

Safety & health management was as crucial skill of steel reinforced concrete project.(Parts of facilities).

圖 686　鋼骨構架組裝作業中張掛全幕式防墜安全網

Figure 686. safety nets were stretched & tighten to full cover the steel structure to prevent the fall accident during the assembly work.

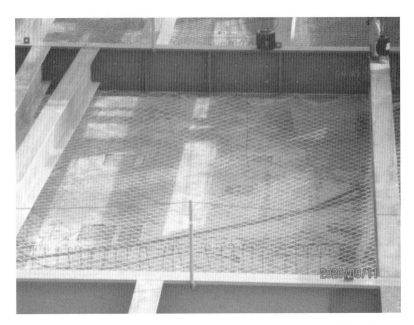

圖 687　鋼骨構架柱樑組立為成框架時，必須先行張掛防墜安全網。

Figure 687. Safety nets should be stretched & tied when column & beam assembly joined as framework completely.

圖 688　鋼構作業俟鋼樓梯組裝完成時，必須先行組裝安全欄杆。

Figure 688. Steel staircase has been mounted completely on the framework that guardrail should erected steady on both side of it.

圖 689　現場電焊作業的工作平台及上下設備垂直護籠均符合安全規定

Figure 689. Fixed ladders with safety cages & work platform were complied the safety regulation for the welding work on the steel structure.

圖 690　電焊作業人員作業時，必須隨身準備車用型滅火器一支以防止火災發生。

Figure 690. Welder should bring the dry powder fire extinguisher as vehicle using type with him that was essential object to prevent the fire accident occurred on fire work.

圖 691　樓板開口處需張掛安全網及安全護欄，防止墜落意外發生。

Figure 691. Hatch of floor slab was installed the guardrail with safety net to prevent the fall accident occurred.

圖 692　電梯豎井防止墜落措施有柵欄設置、上鎖管控和明顯警告標示。

Figure 692. Elevator shaft which fall protective facilities were as follow guard rail、lock controlled & obvious warning notice etc.

圖 693　結構體施工期間，管道間的臨時防墜措施。

Figure 693. Fall protection facility of shaft has been installed completely during the construction method.

圖 694　結構體樓梯完成時，必須安裝安全護欄。

Figure 694. Stairway has been completed of construction method which should install the guard rail of it.

圖 695　泥作粉刷階段改採垂吊防墜網方式來替代安全護欄，防止人員墜落發生。

Figure 695. For the sake of fall prevent at stairway where during the mason method that safety net should be spread from the top floor slab to the below floor slab.

圖 696　樓板的預留孔均完全覆蓋及有明顯的警告標示

Figure 696. Hatche was covered with planks & pasted obevious warning sign on the plank.

圖 697　各樓層均配置掃具供進場作業人員使用，隨時保持作業區的整潔。

Figure 697. Cleaning utensils were supplied on the each floor that was available to clean the debris at workplace befor go off work.

圖 698　室內樓地版進行清潔及整理的態樣

Figure 698. Scene of the floor slab that worker was in progressing the cleaning work as shine & standardization.

圖 699　各樓層均設置簡易式尿筒及泥作用洗滌桶，以維持工區整潔的態樣。

Figure 699. To keeping the tidy environment of work site that installed some initial simple & convenient facilities of urinal & sediment bucket.

圖 700　一樓管道間旁設置送風機，提供地下結構作業新鮮空氣的供給流通量。

Figure 700. There was one set of air blower installed aside the shaft where supplied the fresh air into the work place of basement.

圖 701　下部結構混凝土作業均使用工業用電扇讓作業環境空氣流通

Figure 701. There was one mobile electric fan at site which provided the air in circulationfor the concrete method of substructure.

圖 702　工地變壓器及臨時分電盤均有安全防護設施

Figure 702. There were transformer & distribution panel box which should have the safety protection facilities to that at site.

圖 703　作業人員休憩場所周邊放置環保垃圾桶及菸蒂筒

Figure 703. There was garbage bins as recycling & cigarette butt case installed at workers' recreation area.

圖 704　工地施工升降機操作人員必須由受訓合格者擔任

Figure 704. Certificates of qualifications are required for operators who work on the elevator of work site.

圖 705　施工升降機的桅杆固定架必須定期檢查維修

Figure 705. The mast tower section of elevator which fixed frame was attached to the structure that it was inspected & maintanced in fixed time.

四、鋼骨鋼筋混凝土構築作業階段安衛管理要項（精進的部分）

Safety & health management as crucial skill of steel reinforced concrete work. (Parts of refine).

圖 706　建築物外觀施工架所使用的防塵網要精選網目和色澤使用

Figure 706. Dust nets of scaffold as appearance of building that was selected the mesh & colour for using.

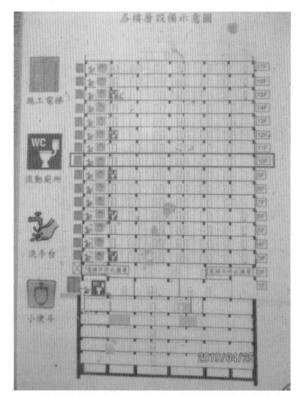

圖 707　標準樓層所規劃的動線及臨時設施的圖示位置圖

Figure 707. Symbal of temporary facilities & access / egress route on the plane in the typical story.

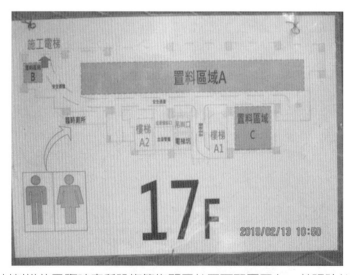

圖 708　材料堆放及臨時廁所設施等均顯示於平面配置圖上，並張貼於樓梯間。

Figure 708. The zone of variety material piling & temporary handable toilet were shown on the floor's layout which was post on the staircase.

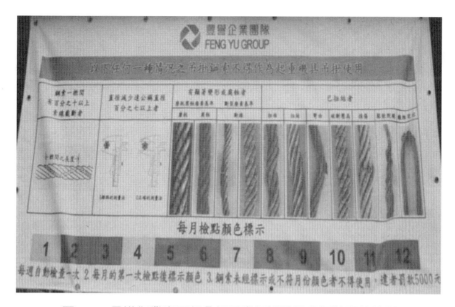

圖 709　吊掛作業索具部分每月進行檢點及色標管理的態樣

Figure 709. Steel wire rope of lifting operation that should been inspected & painted the colour as that month to the wire rope for safety control system.

圖 710　工區的看板內容說明運用優質的管理機制，將工程中研判的風險排除。

Figure 710. Content of billboard as description which executed the superior safety management that was eliminated the potential risk in the work progress.

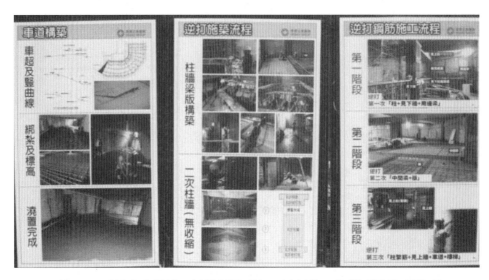

圖 711　看板內容就地下結構採用逆打工法其施工作業重點事項說明

Figure 711. Illustratted the critical working procedure of top-down construction method witch executed in substructure on the billboard.

圖 712　工法展示的深層意義，是作業前已完成危害辨識及施工中的風險評量及對策方法。

Figure 712. Deeply meaning of method which performs was studied of hazard identification in prior work operation & related the risk assessment with the strategy of problems on the billboard perform.

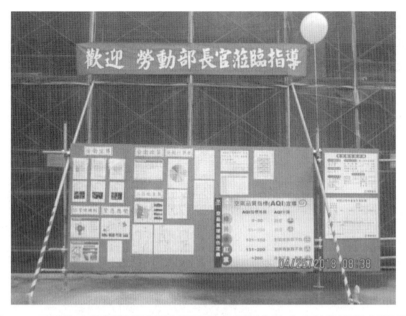

圖 713　工地的安衛優質管理機制及工法的創新作法向來訪的貴賓介紹展示

Figure 713. Premium management of safety &health with innovation construction method were showed & inllustrated to the honored persons that visited at construction site.

圖 714　工地要求施工架廠商到現場先行組裝實體模型，以利相關安全問題的探討。

Figure 714. Scaffold has been erected completion with professional subcontractor that mock up was good for the studing related of safety problem at site.

圖 715　工區周邊的植栽樹木均需用麻布包裹保護

Figure 715. Tree was protected with the wrapped burlap with plants where growed on the pedestrains way aside the construction project area.

6-7 鋼骨結構工程 Steel structure construction

一、何謂鋼骨結構？What is steel structure?

　　鋼骨結構是一種金屬結構，由結構鋼組件相互連接以承載載荷，並提供充分的剛性。由於鋼的強度高，這種結構可靠，與其他類型的結構（如混凝土結構和木材結構）相比，所需的原材料更少。

　　鋼骨結構在現代建築中市場的使用率有愈來愈高的趨勢，鋼結構建築通過使用細長的立柱來最大化建築面積效率，最大化可利用的地面空間，更長的跨度，用於無立柱的開放空間，與同等的混凝土柱相比，典型的鋼柱占用的地面空間要少 75%。同時結構鋼料允許更長的跨度，此特性可讓業主有更大的空間可以規劃使用，從而形成了廠房及開放式辦公室優先考慮的結構設計。

圖 716　重型工業廠房為工期的考量，均採用鋼骨結構設計的態樣。

Figure 716. New factory building was adoppd the steel structure design due to the concern of construction duration.

二、選擇鋼結構構築的 4 個最大誘因？Four reasons of why steel structure is the best choice?

(一) 節省成本 Cost savings

在大多數材料和設計項目中，鋼結構是成本引領者。它的製造和安裝成本低廉，與其他傳統建築方法相比，所需維護更少。

(二) 創造力 Creativity

鋼鐵具有塑性的美，大多數建築師迫不及待地想要利用它的特點。如果您希望創造任何形狀的結構，都可以享受很多的鋼性質樸美。

(三) 控制與管理 Control and management

鋼結構在工廠製造，並由工地熟練的技術人員在吊裝現場進行組裝作業，確保組裝人員在施工過程的安全。不僅作業現場的防墜設施要完整，而且人員的管理機制都必須落實，落實是管理中最佳解決問題的對策。

(四) 耐久性 Durability

它可以承受極端的力量衝擊或惡劣的天氣條件，例如強風、地震、颶風和大雪。如鋼鐵表面加上塗裝，即使使用的年限增加，它們也不易生鏽。

三、鋼骨結構工程階層構築作業概述 Description of steel structure construction was in different layer procedures.

圖 717　工業廠房的鋼構建造面積要寬廣，才能展現鋼構設計的優勢。

Figure 717. There was advantage of steel structure design that was gross construction area should in vast fot the factory build.

圖 718　工程師使用測量儀器把開挖範圍及基樁位置用石灰足尺放樣標示出來

Figure 718. The scope of excavation & piles' location were marked with full scale of lime on the ground that engineer has been used the survey instrument.

圖 719　現場進行開挖後，地下的基樁均完整呈現於地面上的態樣。

Figure 719. There was appeared completely of piles'cap after execavating work at related area in work site.

圖 720　現場破碎機進行破碎樁頭的劣質混凝土

Figure 720. Lean concrete of piles' cap was breaked to debris with concrete breaker at site.

圖 721　現場樁頭的劣質混凝土被破碎後，預留樁主筋的態樣。

Figure 721. Major rebars were retained of the pile cap that portion of lean concrete was breaked with breaker.

圖 722　現場單元組的樁帽混凝土鋪面澆置完成的態樣

Figure 722. There was three piles in a unit which pave of pile caps has been completed for follow-up work.

圖 723　現場樁帽底層鋼筋紮結完成作業的態樣

Figure 723. The rebar work of lower layer ha been completed of pile cap.

圖 724　承商準備的角鋼架於作業現場置放的態樣

Figure 724. There were many pieces of angle steel frames which delivered at site with subcontractor for footing of steel column erecting.

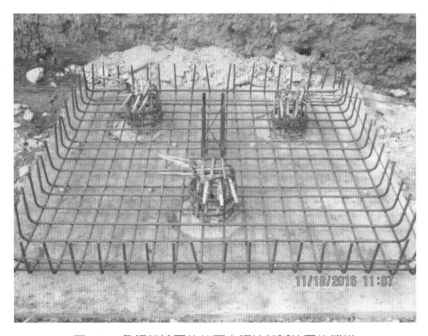

圖 725　角鋼架被置放於獨立鋼柱基腳位置的態樣

Figure 725. There was a piece of angle steel frame which was placed at the footing location

圖 726　單元組的樁帽已完成下層筋紮結及獨立鋼柱基腳的置放依序排列態樣

Figure 726. The rebars work of lower layer of unit pile cap with angle steel frame which was finished to arrange in a line.

圖 727　作業人員於角鋼支撐架上端位置進行定心及高程確認的態樣

Figure 727. Steel worker held the tool on the angle steel frame to fixed position & elevation with surveying instruments.

圖 728　鋼柱的底鈑及預埋螺栓固定於角鋼支撐架上端的態樣

Figure 728. There was steel base plate with 4 pieces of anchor bolts embedded on the top of angle steel frame that has been fixed position & elevation.

圖 729　鋼柱底鈑及預埋螺栓被固定於樁帽基腳鋼筋紮結完成的態樣

Figure 729. There was steel baes plate with 4 pieces of anchor bolts embedded in the pile cap rebar framing.

圖 730　現場樁帽基腳鋼筋紮結完成後，模板組立亦完成的態樣。

Figure 730. Shuttering of pile cap with footing was tight joint with grade nails after the rebar framing has been completed at site.

圖 731　現場樁帽基腳進行混凝土澆置的態樣

Figure 731. Scene of pile cap with footing was placing the concrete in progressing at work site.

圖 732　現場每一單元性的基礎混凝土澆置已完成的態樣

Figure 732. The each unit of foundation which has been placed the concrete completely.

圖 733　單元性的基礎已完成周邊回填土的態樣

Figure 733. Soil has been back filled completely on the rim of each unit foundation.

圖 734　鋼柱吊放於基礎與預埋螺栓結合固定的態樣

Figure 734. Scene of steel column was lifting to steps down in size at the baseplate with nuts to the anchor bolts on the foundation.

圖 735　現場起重機進行鋼樑吊掛組裝的態樣

Figure 735. Scene of crane was lifting operation of steel beam to assemble for steel frame at site in progressing.

圖 736　現場組裝人員使用高空工作車進行柱樑的鎖固作業

Figure 736. Steel worker used the aerial work platform to fasten the column & beam in tight joint.

圖 737　現場鋼構吊掛組裝如形成一個框架時，必須張掛安全防墜網的態樣。

Figure 737. When the steel structure of frame has been fixed in the lifting operation that safety nets should be spreat & tied completely among the space.

圖 738　現場使用滑車吊鏈進行鋼柱垂直度的調整

Figure 738. Workers of steel assembly work that they used the chain block to clamp the steel column which was adjusted the verticality of steel column.

圖 739 現場起重機準備進行鋼構樓梯吊掛組裝的態樣

Figure 739. The crane was ready to lift the steel ladder on the steel frame as designed location in progressing.

圖 740 現場起重機進行鋼構吊掛組裝的態樣

Figure 740. Scene of steel beam has been lifted on the proper location for assembling as steel frame with workers at site.

圖 741　現場鋼構屋頂完成吊掛組裝及安全網張掛完全的態樣

Figure 741. Scene of safety nets has been spreaded all area which below the steel structure frame after roof structure frame was assembled completely.

圖 742　現場鋼承鈑俟鋼筋紮結完成，經技師檢查合格後，進行混凝土的澆置。

Figure 742. Scene of the rebar work has been finished of the deck floor which was examined in qualitied with register engineer then pour concrete to the slab in progressing at site.

圖 743　樓板進行混凝土澆置已完成的範圍於 3 小時後進行整體粉光的態樣

Figure 743. There was finishing concrete with power trowel smooth on thedeck slab where concrete has been placed completely in 3 hours before.

圖 744　樓板完成整體粉光後的態樣

Figure 744. Scene of deck slab where has been finished with the power trowel smooth.

圖 745　屋頂作業進行彩鋼鈑的搬運及安裝固定的態樣

Figure 745. Workers carried away the sheet metal roofing to the position that they fixed the sheet metal in size on the roof work.

圖 746　現場屋頂彩鋼鈑及天窗全部組裝固定於桁條施工完成的態樣

Figure 746. Scene of the sheets metal with skylight panels was mounted & fixed on the purlin of the roof.

圖 747　現場油漆工使用高空工作車進行鋼樑防火材料噴塗作業的態樣

Figure 747. Painter droved the aerial work platform that he spraied the fire resistant paint to the steel beam of steel structure frame.

圖 748　鋼骨結構室內所有作業完成後態樣

Figure 748. Scene of the works has been done in the indoor of the steel structure.

圖 749　鋼構組裝人員使用吊籃進行外牆 C 型槽鋼安裝的態樣

Figure 749. Scene of the Csection girts were fixed in size on the side wall with the steel assembling workers on the lifting cage.

圖 750　鋼構廠房外牆 C 型槽鋼及鋁窗窗框安裝完成的態樣

Figure 750. There were C section girts with several sets of aluminum frames installed completely on exterior wall of steel structure.

圖 751 牆面彩鋼鈑施工人員使用鋁管工作架進行安裝作業的態樣

Figure 751. Scene of workers as team work that they used the aluminum elevated ladder to fixed the metal panels in size on the wall.

圖 752 彩鋼鈑作業使用鋁管工作架，其滑輪座架和角鋼也可安置板材上面移動時用人力推進的態樣。

Figure 752. The angle steel was mounted on the planks which has been laid on the ground that base with fixed pulley of aluminum elevated ladder was on it, which was forwarded by men's force when workers finished the metal panels in size on the wall.

圖 753　鋁管工作架其滑輪座架和角鋼也可安置在混凝土地面上，其行進移位時用人力推送
　　　　的態樣。

Figure 753. The angle steel was laid on the top of concrete that base with fixed pulley of aluminum
elevated ladder was moved forward with manpower for next scope of metal panels work.

圖 754　現場彩鋼鈑安裝人員均穿戴及勾掛背負式安全帶作業的態樣

Figure 754. Scene of workers were to fixed the metal panels on the side wall that are to embressed
harness & used the large snap hook for the work.

圖 755　廠房外牆彩鋼鈑已有部分範圍完成組裝的態樣

Figure 755. Scene of the metal panel has been fixed in some portion of exterior wall in factory building.

四、鋼骨結構構築作業階段安衛管理要項（作業人員的部分）

Safety & health management was crucial skill of steel structure project (Part of access worker).

圖 756　鋼骨結構相關工程作業承商作業主管，接受總承商安排的作業前危害辨識安全教育訓練。

Figure 756. Safety training of hazard identification prior the work operation to supervisors who were subcontractors of steel structure related work that training was provided with general contractor at site meeting room.

圖 757　現場鋼構相關作業人員都需穿戴背負式安全帶

Figure 757. Workers embraced the full body harness for the work of steel structure.

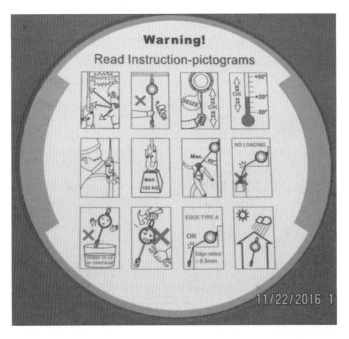

圖 758　使用捲揚防墜器時，必須事先詳讀使用說明及相關象形圖示。

Figure 758. Worker should read the instruction carefully & realized the pictograms completely of Self-Retracting Lifeline (SRL) before using.

圖 759　工地舉辦高空工作車操作安全實地訓練

Figure 759. Safety operation of aerial work platform was held to pratical training to workers with instructor at site.

圖 760　學員依照標準操作程序，實地親自操作高空工作車的態樣。

Figure 760. Scene of trainees operated the aerial work platform which according to the standard operation procedure that trainees were in person to practice.

圖 761　工程師每週定期召開高風險作業的施工風險評估態樣

Figure 761. Scene of construction risk evaluation meeting has been convened & discussed on the fixed date in each week with engineers that they focus to the work of high risk operation.

五、鋼骨結構構築作業階段安衛管理要項（設備的部分）Safety & health management was crucial skill of steel structure project (parts of facility).

圖 762　鋼骨結構構築作業階段防墜安全網均需張掛完全

Figure 762. Steel structure frame has been completed which safety net was spreaded & tied tighten below the slab deck.

圖 763　鋼骨結構外部進行施工架組裝，以利後續牆面構築作業。

Figure 763. Scaffold has been assembled adjacent the steel structure which was benefitted the subsequence work of wall construction.

圖 764　鋼骨結構與施工架需採繫牆桿配合 C 型夾扣，才能防止施工架倒塌。

Figure 764. To prevent the collapse accident that scaffold has to be connected the lower flange of steel beam with metal pipe of C-type clamp & swival clamp.

圖 765　施工架作業人員穿戴背負式安全帶，並勾掛正鋪設截斷層的底鈑態樣。

Figure 765. Workers embressed the full harness & used the snap big hook on the lifeline to place the iron sheets on the bracket of disconnected layer of scaffold.

圖 766　為防止飛落意外發生，施工架需依法設置斜籬防制的態樣。

Figure 766. To prevent falling object that was aerial steel net should be mounted on the scaffold which comply with the regulation.

圖 767　廠房的消防系統吊掛高度超過 10M 均使用高空工作車作業

Figure 767. Hydrant system has been mounted under slab deck which height was over 10 M that worker was operating the aerial work platform to the work.

圖 768　使用高空工作車並載運材料作業時，材料必須綑紮防止飛落。

Figure 768. Material as steel pipe was delieveried with aerial work platform that object should be tied up with worker to prevent the falling accident.

圖 769　作業人員使用高空工作車作業必須穿戴背負式安全帶及使用勾掛

Figure 769. Worker operated the aerial work platform for assembling work that he should embressed the full body harness & attached the snap big hook on the guardrail.

圖 770　作業人員駕駛高空工作車行進前，必須將作業平台下降，防止翻覆意外。

Figure 770. To prevented upside down that aerial work platform should be going down to lowest position before go ahead to another job site with worker operated the vehicle.

圖 771　作業人員使用不同機型的高空工作車作業應保持安全距離

Figure 771. Worker operated the aerial work platform at same working area that worker should keep the safety distance to each others to prevent the accident occure.

六、鋼骨結構構築作業階段安衛管理要項（精進的部分）Safety & health management was crucial skill of steel structure project (parts of refine)

(一) 鋼網牆作業工法 Work method of wall with steel mesh.

圖 772　輕型鋼骨架進場堆放至作業區以便使用的態樣

Figure 772. Scene of light weight steel fram has been placed at job site.

圖 773　電焊人員依照設計圖說進行安裝電焊固定輕型鋼骨架態樣

Figure 773. Base on the plan that light weight steel fram has been welded with welder at job site.

圖 774　水平的加勁鋼筋與垂直輕型鋼骨架相互紮結在一起

Figure 774. Enforceable rebar has een placed on the light weight steel frame which was tied with the verticle pole.

圖 775　輕型鋼骨架與鋼筋紮結，其外部表面將金屬抓漿網電焊固定的態樣。

Figure 775. Steel mesh of motar captured was welded on the exterior surface of light weight steel fram with enforceable rebar.

圖 776　完成室內隔間構築的三要件是輕型鋼骨架鋼筋和金屬抓漿網的態樣

Figure 776. Compartment of indoor has been completed which initial elements were light weight steel fram, rebar & steel mesh as mortar captured.

圖 777　室內隔間的鋼網牆作業完成後，即進行混凝土澆置的樣態。

Figure 777. Pouring the concrete of high flowable concrete (HFC) after the compartment's wall of steel mesh which has been completed.

圖 778　室內隔間牆完成混凝土澆置的樣態

Figure 778. Scene of the indoor compartment where has been finished the pouring concrete completely.

圖 779　室內逃生梯外牆完成混凝土澆置的樣態

Figure 779. Scene of the indoor evacuation stairs where has been finished the pouring concrete completely.

圖 780　室內逃生梯內牆完成灰誌張貼，準備泥作粉刷的樣態。

Figure 780. Scene of indoor evacuation stairs where was the margen has been pasted on the interior wall for the subsequent of mason's work.

圖 781　室內外牆壁進行泥作粉刷的樣態

Figure 781. Scene of mason's work was in progressing for exterior & interior wall at work site.

(二)鋼網系模作業工法 Steel mesh with formwork systemwork method.

圖 782　室內隔間牆將採用新工法，即所謂鋼網系模作業工法的樣態。

Figure 782. New work method of steel mesh with formwork system which was adapted to the work of indoor compartment.

圖 783　室内隔間牆的結構安全行為將採用鋼網牆方式作業

Figure 783. The work method would be fabricated to steel meth wall for the manner of safety structure to the wall of indoor compartment.

圖 784　結構鋼網牆施作完成後，外部採系統模板封模作業。

Figure 784. The steel mesh has been fabricated completely in the middle of wall then formwork system was installed to both side of wall surface.

圖 785　結構鋼網系統模板拆模後，牆面呈現平滑的態樣。

Figure 785. The wall surface performed the even & smooth after wall panel of formwork system was dismantled at site.

6-8 創改型系統模板工程 Creation & improvement type of formwork system construction.

　　台商回流蓋廠及民間房市升溫，全台營建業卻陷入「百年大缺工」的窘境，所謂「有錢也找無工」。

　　所謂「山不轉路轉，路不轉人轉，人不轉心轉」，創改及創新工法是業界扭轉當今危機變成轉機的對策之一，採用系統模板的材料及相關配件為基本的必要條件，但傳統結構的鋼筋組紮作業，配合不同系統模板的材料使用，我們公司秉持多年來在業界的口碑，對於任何工法的突破，進而達到創改及創新的層面來造福社會，也是敝公司領導階層近年來訂定的政策之一。

一、系統模板之優點 Advantage of formwork system

　　(一) 工期短 Short period of construction：系統模板通常具備簡易拆裝之功能設計，並可減少諸多假設工程，施工週期亦不受氣候影響且可循環作業，如此一來便可達到有效縮短工期之好處。

　　(二) 長期經營成本低 Low cost of long term running：系統模板通常可重複使用，具有高度經濟價值，亦可省下許多人力資源，且作業便利又能縮短工期，效率高，初期成本雖高，但長期經營成本卻相對划算。

　　(三) 提高建築物品質 Improve the quality of construction：因材料模具化、施作技術標準

化，對於品質掌控便可更加精確，有效解決工人素質良莠不齊、材料堆放不善導致工作效益低落及傳統模板拆模後常有殘留物之問題，進而提升建築物之品質。

(四) 安全 Safety：系統模板無須如傳統模板必須以電鋸分別截割各單位所需之尺寸，亦無須攀高組立模板，可達到施工更安全之效益。

(五) 環保 Recycling：系統模板使用之材料，大多為環保材質，不僅可重複利用，並且皆具有可回收再利用性質，且無須如傳統模板裁切木材，便可減少建築施工中的廢棄物，達到環保的效益。

二、系統模板之缺點 Disadvantage of formwork system

(一) 初期成本高。High cost in primary stage.

(二) 不適合小型工程。Small scale of construction was unsuited for.

(三) 無法用於複雜之結構體施工。Panel of form system was not fitted to complex construction method.

(四) 事前需培訓施工人員之專業能力。Training of installing process for the skilled worker prior the work on commences.

整體而言，系統模板的發明不僅對建築物本身品質有正向效益，長期而言，對於營建業者也有較好的經濟價值，同時又能兼顧勞工的權益，尤其是勞工安全層面；透過系統模板我們發現只要有心，便可以創造改變，不僅讓建築工法更完善，甚至可以達到讓業主、承造商及勞工三贏的局面。

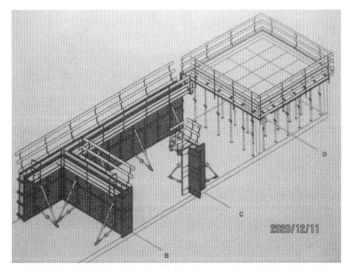

圖 786　組成態樣說明使用系統模板組立柱、牆、版的作業程序有許多特點
Figure 786. Configuration was performed the particular of column、wall & slab which install with the panel of formwork system at work site.

圖 787　系統模板放在集裝架上，安全地被運送到工地的態樣。

Figure 787. Panel of formwork was stacked on the pallet which has been delivered at work site in safety.

圖 788　作業人員進行系統模板面板清理以備使用的態樣

Figure 788. Workers cleaned the surface of panel prior which was utilized at job site.

圖 789　系統模板面板清理後，均勻塗抹脫模劑後晾乾的態樣。

Figure 789. The release agent was applied uniformly on the surface of panel of form work & dry in the air at job site.

圖 790　現場作業人員進行系統模板面板尺寸量測的態樣

Figure 790. Scene of worker measured the size of panel of form work to assembly.

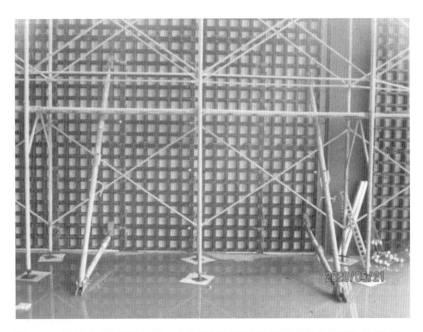

圖 791　依據作業流程，第一階牆壁面板組裝需裝置鋼管斜撐的態樣。

Figure 791. According the work procedure that push-pull prop with base plate was mounted on the concrete floor on the panel assembly in first phase.

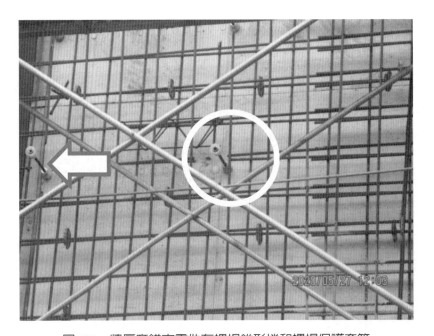

圖 792　牆厚度錨定零件有螺桿錐形擋和螺桿保護套等

Figure 792. The required components as anchor system include load of rod, cones of both side & spacer tube etc.

圖 793　現場牆壁面板依照規範裝置鋼管斜撐，防止倒塌意外發生的態樣。

Figure 793. Scene of panel form has been installed which height meets the specification that push-pull prop was mounted on the floor to prevented the collapse accident occurred.

圖 794　現場牆壁使用系統模板封模完成後，進行混凝土澆置完成的態樣。

Figure 794. Scene of concrete has been poured into the rebar frame between the panel system forms.

圖 795　現場作業人員進行單元性系統模板接合器向上旋轉鬆開拆卸的態樣

Figure 795. Worker was doing the dismantle work at job site that standard panel joint of couplers has been gripped with hand & swiveled upwards to lose it.

圖 796　現場作業人員進行單元性系統模板拆卸的態樣

Figure 796. Standard panel unit has been moved after couplers of panel joint were released in completely.

圖 797　現場作業人員於牆壁系統模板拆除後，進行混凝土表面的修飾態樣。

Figure 797. Workers were decorated the joint place where oddments were stroked off after the panel form unit has been disassembly.

圖 798　第一階牆壁裝置三角架，以利隨後系統模板組裝作業時供鋼管斜撐固定。

Figure 798. Triangle brackets were mounted on the wall as concrete in 1st phase finished, that benefit to the connected of push-pull prop for subsequent process.

圖 799　作業人員進行第二階牆壁系統模板升高組裝作業的態樣

Figure 799. Scene of worker has been assembled the stand panel for the second construction in height.

圖 800　施工架組裝需注意鋼管斜撐的穩定及系統模板組裝作業時的安全性

Figure 800. During scaffold assembly was approached the formwork system that workers should beware the steady of shore system & safety to wall panel assembly.

圖 801　要求施工架人員增加下翼鈑繫牆桿的數量，防止施工架倒塌意外發生。

Figure 801. Workers of scaffold assembling were requested that mounted to the bottom flange of steel beam as C-type clamp with pipe to connect scaffold which quantity should be prepared more than normal situation for safety consideration.

圖 802　上一階牆壁系統模板混凝土澆置完成且部分拆模後的態樣

Figure 802. Some scope of panel system which has been dismantled of upper construction height after concrete finished the pouring work.

圖 803　因應系統模板高架作業施工架組裝的上下設備應符合安全規定

Figure 803. Scaffold assembled with access ladder that should comply to the safety regulation for the formwork system in upper construction as required of design.

圖 804　系統鋁模放在集裝架上，安全被運送到工地的態樣。

Figure 804. Al-formwork system was stacked on the pallet which has been delivered at work site in safety.

圖 805　作業人員正進行系統鋁模表面均勻塗抹脫模劑的態樣

Figure 805. Worker was applying uniformly the form oil on the each panel of Al-formwork system at job site.

圖 806　創新的框式鋼筋組紮工法被運用在結構外牆系統鋁模作業的態樣

Figure 806. The creation working method of rebar work as frame has been applied to the exterior wall of Al-formwork system method.

圖 807　鋼筋工正進行結構外牆框式鋼筋組紮作業的態樣

Figure 807. Rebar workers were too installed & tied the rebar with steel frame on the exterior wall.

圖 808　依照模組計畫，作業人員正進行牆面單元鋁模的內角扣件安裝作業之態樣。

Figure 808. Wall panels were assembled in completed that worker inserted the in corner (IC) on each panel which based on the form plan.

圖 809　鋁模工正進行結構外牆鋁模安裝的態樣

Figure 809. Al-form has been assembled on the designed area of exterior wall.

圖 810　外牆鋁模安裝加勁橫擋及固定夾鉗的態樣

Figure 810. There was a compensation steel wale nipped with clamp on the Al-form of exterior wall.

圖 811　第一階外牆鋁模全部安裝完成及外模斜撐架也已固定的態樣

Figure 811. Position wall panel of Al-form in 1st phase has been assembled completely with the push-pull props which steady on the concrete floor.

圖 812　第一階外牆鋁模全部安裝完成進行混凝土澆置的態樣

Figure 812. Position wall panel of Al-form has been assembled completely then concrete pouring work was in progressing.

圖 813　混凝土澆置完成後，進行牆面鋁模拆除的態樣。

Figure 813. Wall panel of Al-form has been dismantled completely to each unit after concrete pouring work was finished.

圖 814　作業人員使用高空工作車進行上一階鋁模外牆組裝的態樣

Figure 814. Workers drove the aerial work platform that they were to set up the upper Al-formwork on exterior wall.

圖 815　作業人員使用施工架進行上一階鋁模外牆組裝的態樣

Figure 815. Workers used the scaffold that they were to set up the upper Al-formwork on exterior wall in progressing at site.

圖 816　鋁模進行柱牆組裝，為防止倒塌意外，伸縮性斜撐必須固定於牆面。

Figure 816. Wall & column has been installed of Al-formwork which height fit in designed requirement that push-pull props should mount to the wall to prevent the collapse accident occurred.

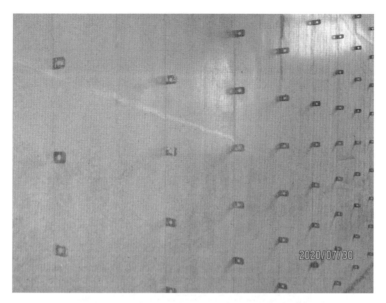

圖 817　現場室內牆壁的系統鋁模拆模後，內角扣件殘留在牆壁的態樣。

Figure 817. Scene of Al-form has been dismantled of indoor wall that was lot of in corner (IC) has remained on the wall.

圖 818　外牆系統鋁模拆模後，內角扣件殘留在牆壁的態樣。

Figure 818. There were lots of in corner (IC) has remained on the wall after Al-form has been dismantled of outdoor wall.

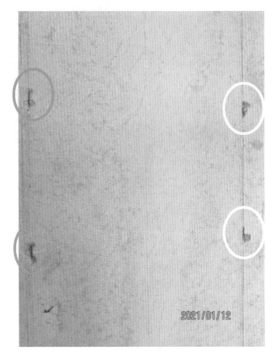

圖 819　牆壁的內角扣件被折斷部位的態樣

Figure 819. Scene of the position which was the in corner (IC) has been broken away on the wall.

圖 820　牆壁的內角扣件折斷後，其破口部位被補平的態樣。

Figure 820. Scene of the position which was the in corner (IC) has been broken away where concave was fix to the flat smooth on the wall.

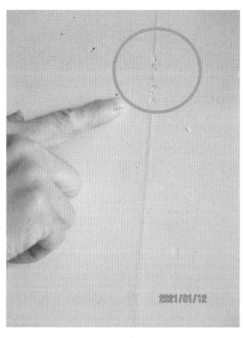

圖 821　牆壁內角扣件破口部位補平處需打磨後，才能進行油漆作業。

Figure 821. Grinding work to the concave position where has been finished then the painting is in working on the wall.

圖 822　作業人員正進行牆面鋁模的整體分類及堆放作業的態樣

Figure 822. Worker moved the Al-form panel in sort out of size & stacked the same panel unit in together.

圖 823　現場多餘鋁模依型號尺寸分類堆放的態樣

Figure 823. Redundant Al-form panel has been arranged in sort out of size & model number which stacked the same panel unit in together at site.

圖 824　多餘的鋁模依尺寸暫時堆放，準備運離工區的態樣。

Figure 824. Redundant Al-form panel has been arranged in fix area with temporary warning facilities which were delivered by truck out from the site.

國家圖書館出版品預行編目資料

工事安全衛生精實管理／彭元傑作. －－初
版.－－臺北市：五南圖書出版股份有限公
司，2022.02
面； 公分
ISBN 978-626-317-537-2 (平裝)

1.CST：工業安全 2.CST：職業衛生

555.56 110022826

5T53

工事安全衛生精實管理

作 者 — 彭元傑（278.4）

發 行 人 — 楊榮川

總 經 理 — 楊士清

總 編 輯 — 楊秀麗

副總編輯 — 王正華

責任編輯 — 張維文

封面設計 — 姚孝慈

出 版 者 — 五南圖書出版股份有限公司

地 址：106台北市大安區和平東路二段339號4樓

電 話：(02)2705-5066 傳 真：(02)2706-6100

網 址：https://www.wunan.com.tw

電子郵件：wunan@wunan.com.tw

劃撥帳號：01068953

戶 名：五南圖書出版股份有限公司

法律顧問 林勝安律師事務所 林勝安律師

出版日期 2022年2月初版一刷

定 價 新臺幣600元

經典永恆・名著常在

五十週年的獻禮——經典名著文庫

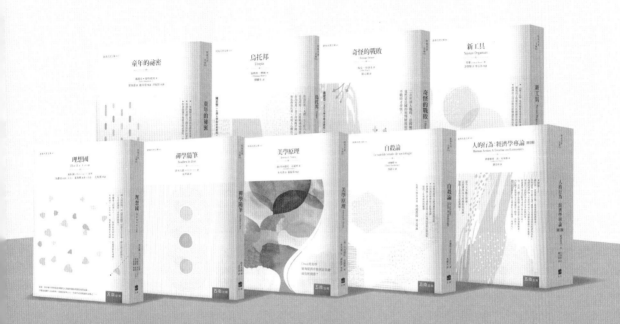

五南，五十年了，半個世紀，人生旅程的一大半，走過來了。

思索著，邁向百年的未來歷程，能為知識界、文化學術界作些什麼？

在速食文化的生態下，有什麼值得讓人雋永品味的？

歷代經典・當今名著，經過時間的洗禮，千錘百鍊，流傳至今，光芒耀人；

不僅使我們能領悟前人的智慧，同時也增深加廣我們思考的深度與視野。

我們決心投入巨資，有計畫的系統梳選，成立「經典名著文庫」，

希望收入古今中外思想性的、充滿睿智與獨見的經典、名著。

這是一項理想性的、永續性的巨大出版工程。

不在意讀者的眾寡，只考慮它的學術價值，力求完整展現先哲思想的軌跡；

為知識界開啟一片智慧之窗，營造一座百花綻放的世界文明公園，

任君遨遊、取菁吸蜜、嘉惠學子！